Points of View in Writing

domains
in language and composition

Points
of View
in Writing

Edward B. Jenkinson
Donald A. Seybold

Harcourt Brace Jovanovich, Inc.
New York Chicago San Francisco Atlanta Dallas

EDWARD B. JENKINSON is Associate Professor of Education, Co-ordinator for School English Language Arts, and Director of the Indiana University English Curriculum Study Center. In 1970-71 he was Vice President of the National Council of Teachers of English. Professor Jenkinson has written and edited several books on the teaching of high school language and literature and is the author of *People, Words, and Dictionaries,* another *Domains in Language and Composition* book.

DONALD A. SEYBOLD is Assistant Director of the Indiana University English Curriculum Study Center. With Professor Jenkinson, he is coauthor of *Writing as a Process of Discovery.*

ISBN 0-15-312327-3

ACKNOWLEDGMENTS: *For permission to reprint copyrighted material, grateful acknowledgment is made to the following sources:*

ART BUCHWALD: "Hey Tovarich, Honey: The Fashion Gap Is Showing" by Art Buchwald from *The Courier-Journal & Times,* Louisville, Kentucky, November 8, 1970, copyright © 1970 by Art Buchwald.

FARRAR, STRAUS & GIROUX, INC.: "The Lottery" by Shirley Jackson, copyright 1948, 1949 by Shirley Jackson.

BARTHOLD FLES, LITERARY AGENT: "The New Kid" by Murray Heyert from *Harper's* Magazine, June 1944, copyright © 1944, by Minneapolis Star and Tribune Co., Inc.

FUNK & WAGNALLS COMPANY: Definition of "Society" from Funk & Wagnalls Standard® College Dictionary, copyright © 1968 and previous copyrights 1963, 1966 by Funk & Wagnalls.

ALFRED A. KNOPF, INC.: From *The Autobiography of an Ex-Coloured Man,* by James Weldon Johnson, copyright 1927 by Alfred A. Knopf, Inc.; and renewed 1955 by Carl Van Vechten. From *The Light in the Forest,* by Conrad Richter, copyright 1953 by Conrad Richter, copyright 1953 by The Curtis Publishing Co.

iv

Contents

Chapter 1

A Matter of Time, a Matter of Age

An Editorial

The "now generation" rioted last week at Central High School. The coddled, insubordinate, undisciplined products of permissive parents threw a few rocks at windows and hurled a lot of obscenities down the halls. Shouting for their rights, these soft-headed downgraders of democracy, wearing skirts too short and pants too tight, demonstrated once more that they know little about this great nation, less about history, and nothing about anything that really matters.

What turned the rockheads on this time? The rockheads turned on when the rock music turned off. Principal George Stoneright unplugged the jukebox in the cafeteria after observing what he called "lewd dancing" by some students. The acidheads popped off. They want their coke and rock, too, they said.

According to the police, at least forty students roamed through the halls, shouting the four-letter words so typical of these tele-vocabulary brats. Four of the teen-age hoods were arrested for breaking windows. Like their pseudointellectual older brothers and sisters who are befouling college campuses with dirty language and dirty bodies, the four arrested hoodlums demanded amnesty even before they were booked by the police.

What is this "now generation" anyway? What have we parents unleashed on the world? These kids play the game of being radical so long as we parents pamper them. They don't work; they just sit around and plot riots. They want us to give them money to put gas in their sports cars; money to buy the latest long-playing noise from some filthy, loud, no-talent group of bums; money to take some long-haired, short-skirted sexpot to the latest dirty movie; and money to buy greasy hamburgers for their phony revolutionary bellies.

These kids play at everything. They don't read; they won't read. Perhaps they can't read. They just want to look at pictures, listen to the drum-thumping and tuneless caterwauling they call music, boast about how much they think they know about the world, and cry for mercy the minute they do something like rioting, which they think is heroic.

We wonder how these sniveling smart alecks can really be sons and daughters of the heroes who saved this country in World War II. The parents of these kids weren't pampered. They never questioned what they were told in school or in the home; they helped make this country great. We could count on their parents. We can't count on the kids of the "now generation" unless their parents really get tough with them and turn them into something besides unkempt, uncouth, unpatriotic boobs. Let's quit pampering the "now generation." It's time to use the rod; the child's already spoiled.

Discussion

How did you feel as you read the editorial? Did you get angry? Why? Analyze your response by answering the following questions:

1. What words, phrases, or sentences particularly upset or pleased me? Why?
2. What kind of person wrote the editorial? Why do I think so? Does he know what is going on in the teen-age world? Why or why not?
3. Do I think the editorial writer made some charges against my generation that are not true? Which words, phrases, or sentences carry charges about my generation that I think are not true? Why do I think they are false? What evidence can I give to prove the statements are false?

Writing Assignment 1

Write a letter to the writer of this editorial, telling him what you believe. Just reread the editorial and then react to it. Say whatever you want to say. Don't worry about your language. Just tell him why you think he's wrong or right. Tell him how you reacted to his editorial. Tell him what you think about *him*. Tell him what you think about adults who think the way he does, if you believe that many adults think the way the writer of this editorial apparently does.

A Second Look

After you have written your response to the writer of the editorial, reread the editorial, and also reread your response before answering the following questions:

1. Why did the editorial upset me? Can I pinpoint two or three things (such as particularly offensive words) that caused me to get angry?
2. Did I become upset because the writer of the editorial made sweeping statements that might be true of several people but not of an entire generation? Was I troubled by such generalizations (sweeping statements) as this one: "They don't work; they just sit around and plot riots"?
3. In my response to the editorial, did I intentionally use words to make the writer of the editorial angry or to show him exactly what I think of him? What words or phrases did I use for that purpose?
4. Did I unintentionally use words that might make the writer angry? What words, phrases, or sentences would make me angry if I were the editorial writer? Why?
5. Did I make generalizations in my response? If so, what are they? Did I support my generalizations with any statements to prove that the generalizations are true?
6. As I responded, in what way did I feel that I was looking at the problems of the "now generation" differently from the writer of the editorial? Explain your answer.

Writing Assignment 2

The editor of your local daily newspaper has given you the opportunity to explain the "now generation" to the readers of the newspaper. Write an article in which you tell the adult subscribers to that newspaper what you think your generation believes in: what they do, what they are. Remember that you are writing mainly for adults. Your purpose in writing is to explain what you think your generation represents, and to write so convincingly that the adult readers of the newspaper will be persuaded to think about and consider your point of view the next time they read an editorial like "Let's Quit Pampering the 'Now Generation.'"

How can you best go about accomplishing the purpose of your article? What can you say to adults to explain your point of view?

As you prepare to write your article, consider the following questions:

1. Is there such a thing as the "now generation"? If so, how can I define it for, or describe it to, an adult audience? If I feel there is no such thing as the "now generation," or if I do not like the label "now generation," what label would I use to describe it? Or do I prefer that no labels be pinned on my generation? Why or why not?
2. What valid generalizations can I make about today's teen-agers? What specific supporting evidence can I give to back up my generalizations? If I cannot offer support for a generalization, is it still valid? What kind of generalization or information about today's teen-agers is likely to be most effective in presenting my case to an adult audience?
3. What misconceptions about teen-agers do I feel are most generally held by adults? How can I deal with these misconceptions to show that they are false? What facts do I have to disprove the misconceptions?
4. Is there any truth to any of the charges made in the editorial or in those statements about my generation that are made by adults and/or newspapers, magazines, radio, and television? If some of those statements are true, how can I answer them? Should I answer them or simply ignore them and deal with the statements that are untrue?

5. Is it possible to speak accurately about a whole generation? Is it possible to look at a few individuals and then make valid generalizations about a whole generation? Do any generalizations about a large group take into account the traits and characteristics of individuals in the group? When I use phrases like all teen-agers or most teen-agers do this or that or think this way or that way, can I back up such statements with strong supporting evidence?

GENERATION GAPS

Every generation seems to have its gaps. From the time of the early Greeks, people have expressed concern about differences of opinion between the young and the old. New ideas, new words, and new fashions have always driven a wedge between generations. The size of the wedge seems to depend on how vocal both young and old are in calling attention to the gap.

Today's so-called generation gap has received a great deal of publicity. Newspapers and radio and television stations call attention to the gap almost daily; magazines publish articles on the differences between youth and age in today's world. Books and movies sometimes emphasize the points that separate the young and the old. But just how wide is the gap? Do you believe there is a serious gap between generations?

Before you answer, carefully consider the following questions and suggestions.

1. Do my parents (or other adults) and I have sharply different opinions about
   teen-age dating
   teen-age fashions
   the eighteen-year-old voting age
   the importance of an education
   religion
   racial issues
   politics
   America's involvement in other countries of the world
   the environment
   contemporary movies and books

2. If my parents (or other adults) and I share approximately the same opinions on each of those issues, why do we? If we have sharply different opinions, why do we?
3. Analyze as many issues as you can on which you and your parents (or other adults) agree. Why does there seem to be agreement? Then analyze as many issues as you can on which you and your parents (or other adults) disagree. Why does there seem to be disagreement? List as many reasons as you can for agreement or disagreement.

Writing Assignment 3

After you have carefully examined the issues on which your parents (or other adults) and you agree or disagree, write a letter to a friend your age and explain in detail why you think there is or is not a generation gap in your family.

Chapter 2

The View from Here

WHERE DO YOU SIT?

Everyone in the bleachers stood to see the play. With thirty seconds showing on the scoreboard clock, Central scored to pull within one point of Northside. A two-point conversion would give Central the game and the conference championship.

Matt held his breath. Standing on tiptoes on the bleacher seat, he strained to see the play seventy yards down the field.

"Why does every big play have to happen at the other end of the field?" he mumbled.

"Shut up and watch the game," Bruce snapped.

"What's going on?" Cindy asked.

"The quarterback's either going to run the ball or pass for two points," Bruce said.

"Why?" Cindy asked.

"So we'll win; that's why," Bruce nearly shouted. Dumb girl, he thought. Why did you want to come to the game anyway?

Central broke from the huddle and lined up in a split T. Matt could barely hear the quarterback bark the signals even though the fans were silent. Matt wished he had Bruce's field glasses, but he knew better than to ask for them now. The quarterback looked as if he were only a foot tall from where Matt stood.

The snap. Quickly the quarterback faded back from the line, cocking his arm for the pass. It was a perfect pass—low but perfect. The tight end dove for the ball in the end zone.

"He made it!" Matt screamed.

"Oh, what do you know, dummy," Bruce shouted. "Can't you see that the idiot trapped the ball?"

"Did we win?" Cindy asked.

Matt wanted to scream at both of them, but then he saw the referee's signal. No good. The quarterback's gamble hadn't paid off. Central was behind by one point, and the clock was running out.

"Where's your glasses, ref?" Matt yelled.

"That's dumb," Bruce muttered. "The end trapped the ball."

"Oh, shut up," Matt screamed. As far as he was concerned, the referee was still blind. Central had lost, and it was all the referee's fault. Matt knew the end had caught the ball. He had to. Central had to win. They just had to win! Anyway, from where he stood, it sure did look good.

Cindy sat down. She wanted to cry, but she knew that her big brother would tease her if she did. And he probably wouldn't take her to another football game. This was her first high school game. Bruce had told Dad he would take his seventh-grade sister to the game so that he could use the car. She bit her lip to keep from crying. Why do we have to lose my first game? she wondered. What's it all about, anyway? she asked herself. Will I ever understand football?

Discussion

1. Cindy, Matt, and Bruce saw the same play from the same position in the bleachers. But did each see it the same way? Explain your answer.
2. Bruce had field glasses and could see the play better than Matt. Could he see the play as well as the referee who called the pass incomplete? Did Bruce see the play from the same angle as the referee? Explain your answer.
3. Why did Matt yell, "Where's your glasses, ref?" What influenced the way Matt saw the play?
4. Why do you think Cindy asked the questions she did? Why do you think Bruce thought, "Dumb girl. Why did you want to come to the game anyway?" Is Cindy *dumb*? Explain your answer.
5. Who do you think saw the play most accurately? Why?

Writing Assignment 1

Write several paragraphs explaining why you do not see a football, basketball, baseball, or hockey game exactly the same way as the following people do:

a person rooting for the same team as you but sitting twenty feet away from you

a person on the other side of the playing field (or playing floor) who is rooting for the other team

the coach of your team

the referee

one of the players

Before you begin writing, you might want to answer the following questions:

1. Why does where I sit at a ball game make a difference in how I see the game?
2. What do I know about the game I am describing? Have I seen a number of games? Do I know all the rules? Why do I go to games? Does my knowledge of the game, or lack of it, affect what I see?
3. What are some of the reasons why the referee and I see the game differently? Does he feel the same as I do about the team I am rooting for? Why, or why not?
4. Do I see the game the same way the coach does? Do I see it the same way one of the players sees it? If not, what are some of the reasons for the differences?

From Different Angles

Automobile accidents are, unfortunately, a very common occurrence in the United States. Perhaps you have had the misfortune of seeing one or, worse, of being in one. What did you see? What do you remember? How many cars were involved? Why did they collide? Who was at fault?

Questions like those are often asked after an automobile accident, and the answers to them are frequently confusing or even misleading. To help you discover why, you might want to perform the following experiment in class:

1. Four students bring to class toy automobiles, preferably self-propelled with batteries or friction motors, and the

class makes the outline of several streets on the floor with chalk or easily-removable masking tape.

2. The class decides which streets are through streets and what the speed limits (according to the speeds of the self-propelled cars) should be. The four students who brought the cars rehearse several times, running the cars at different speeds and timing them so at least two will crash.

3. Then the teacher invites four students from another class to watch the experiment. The visiting students are told the traffic rules and are given a demonstration of the speed laws. (Two of the cars should be faster than the others. They are exceeding the speed limit.) The visitors are asked to sit or stand in different places around the room to watch the cars. Immediately after the crash, each of them writes a report of what happened. You and the members of your class also report what happened, making certain that you write about the crash that occurred when the visitors were present—not the crash that occurred during the rehearsal.

4. The teacher reads the four visitors' reports to the class. You compare the reports with your own. How do they differ? Why do they differ?

5. The teacher invites four more students into the room to watch the cars. This time the class tells the visitors that the cars are being driven by certain people in the community. Make certain at least one of the cars is allegedly driven by someone the visitors like very much and that one is driven by a person they dislike.

6. Again, each of the visitors is asked to write a report of what happened. The teacher reads them to the class. How do the reports of the first group of visitors differ from those of the second group? How does the naming of imaginary drivers affect the reports of the second group? How were the reports of the accident affected by the group's like or dislike of the imaginary drivers?

Perhaps this experiment seems too complex. If so, what experiment can you and your classmates design to accomplish the same thing? After discussing the purpose of the foregoing experiment, think up a less complicated one that will show how both a person's physical vantage point and his emotions affect his point of view.

What's in the Picture?

You probably have had the experience of looking at a picture or a painting with a friend and discovering that the two of you did not see exactly the same thing. Perhaps you noticed more details than your friend did; perhaps you liked the picture and your friend did not; perhaps you were not impressed by the picture or painting and your friend was. Perhaps you knew more about the picture or painting than your friend did.

No two people view anything exactly the same way. Some people spot more details than others. Some people become more emotional about almost everything they see than others do. And some people simply see better than others.

To help you determine how well you and other people see things, you might want to conduct the following experiments:

1. Select a picture from a magazine or newspaper and show it to a friend for thirty seconds. Then ask him or her to tell you what is in the picture.
2. Have your friend show you a picture for thirty seconds. You tell him what's in the picture.
3. Select a picture or a painting you like and show it to a friend. Ask why he likes or dislikes it. Then ask your friend to show you a picture or painting he likes. Why do you like or dislike it? What are some of the reasons for your agreement or disagreement?
4. Watch a small portion of a television news program with a friend. Then turn off the set and write down what you saw. Compare it with what your friend saw. How does your account differ from his? Why do you think the accounts differ?
5. Perform experiment 4 with a person at least twenty years older than you. Do the accounts differ? If so, give as many reasons as you can for the differences.
6. Watch a television quiz show with a friend. Select a quiz show in which there are at least three contestants. Which one do you want to win? Which one does your friend want to win? What are the reasons why you selected a certain contestant? What are your friend's reasons?

Writing Assignment 2

Write a theme in which you analyze why you wanted a certain contestant on a quiz show to win. Give as many reasons for your choice as you can. What made you like the person? What facial expressions or mannerisms did you like? Were you reminded of someone you know? If so, what bearing did that resemblance have on your wanting the contestant to win?

Also explain why you wanted one of the contestants to lose. Did you possibly know a person who looks like that contestant? If so, did that resemblance affect your wanting the contestant to lose?

How much did you know about the contestant you wanted to win? About the contestant you wanted to lose? To what extent did that information affect your choices?

THREE FACTORS
INFLUENCING POINT OF VIEW

As you know, the *vantage point* from which you see an event makes a great deal of difference in what you will see. Your *knowledge* of the event (or your lack of it, as the case may be) also affects your point of view, as does the degree of your *emotional involvement*. That third factor, *emotion*, frequently distorts what you see, hear, say, or do. Consider what happens when you are angry, for example. Do you think clearly? Do you see everything that happens around you? Do you behave the same way you would if you were not angry?

Or consider how you behave when you dislike someone. Do you accept his actions the same way you accept those of someone you like? Do you react to what a person you dislike says the same way you react to the words of a person you like? How does your liking or disliking a person affect your point of view?

Writing Assignment 3

Describe an argument, accident, fight, or game in which you were directly involved in such a manner that your reader, a person your age, will accept your version of what happened.

From whose vantage point will you try to make your reader see the incident you describe? Why?

How much will you tell your reader about the incident? How many and what kind of details will you include? Why?

Will you give your reader only facts about the incident? Or will you also convey your feelings about what happened? Why? Will you give him all the facts? Or will you give him only those that present your point of view?

Writing Assignment 4

Rewrite the description of the argument, accident, fight, or game in which you were involved. In this account, give your reader, a person in authority, all the facts. Do not omit any important details, and do not insert your opinions into your description.

Your purpose here is not to persuade your reader to accept your point of view, but to give him a factual, detailed account of the incident.

After you have completed this assignment, compare it with the version you wrote for Assignment 3. How do they differ? Why do they differ?

Chapter 3

The Insider, The Outsider

"LOSER OF THE CHOOSE-UP"

Did you ever feel uncomfortable because you were smaller than the other kids in your neighborhood or school? Or because you were "big for your age"? Or because you had lots of freckles on your nose? Or because you wore hand-me-down clothes? Or because you felt you weren't pretty or handsome?

Were you ever made fun of or left out of a game because you couldn't play very well? Were you ever the "loser of the choose-up"?

If you had one of these problems, how did it affect the way you thought of yourself? How did it affect the way other people treated you?

Did your "handicap"—if you felt it truly was a handicap —keep you from joining a certain group at school or in the neighborhood? Could you do anything to overcome your "handicap"? Or did you wait for "the new kid" to come along to help you solve your problems as Marty does in the following story?

The New Kid

by Murray Heyert

1   By the time Marty ran up the stairs, past the dentist's office, where it smelled like the time his father was in the hospital, past the fresh paint smell, where the new kid lived, past the garlic smell in 2D; and waited for Mommer to open the door; and threw his schoolbooks on top of the old newspapers that were piled on the sewing machine in the hall; and drank his glass of milk ("How many times

must I tell you not to gulp! Are you going to stop gulping like that or must I smack your face!"); and set the empty glass in the sink under the faucet; and changed into his brown sneakers; and put trees into his school shoes ("How many times must I talk to you! When will you learn to take care of your clothes and not make me follow you around like this!"); and ran downstairs again, past the garlic and the paint and the hospital smells; by the time he got into the street and looked breathlessly around him, it was too late. The fellows were all out there, all ready for a game, and just waiting for Eddie Deakes to finish chalking a base against the curb.

2   Running up the street with all his might, Marty could see that the game would start any minute now. Out in the gutter Paulie Dahler was tossing high ones to Ray-Ray Stickerling, whose father was a bus driver and sometimes gave the fellows transfer so they could ride free. The rest were sitting on the curb, waiting for Eddie to finish making the base and listening to Gelberg, who was a Jew, explain what it meant to be *bar mizvah'd,* like he was going to be next month.

They did not look up as Marty galloped up to them all out of breath. Eddie finished making his base and, after looking at it critically a moment with his head on one side, moved down toward the sewer that was home plate and began drawing a scoreboard alongside it. With his nose running from excitement, Marty trotted over to him.

3   "Just going to play with two bases?" he said, wiping his nose on the sleeve of his lumber jacket, and hoping with all his might that Eddie would think he had been there all the while and was waiting for a game like all the other fellows.

Eddie raised his head and saw that it was Marty. He gave Marty a shove. "Why don't you watch where you're walking?" he said. "Can't you see I'm making a scoreboard?"

He bent over again and with his chalk repaired the line that Marty had smudged with his sneakers. Marty hopped around alongside him, taking care to keep his feet off the chalked box. "Gimme a game, Eddie?" he said.

4   "What are you asking me for?" Eddie said without looking up. "It ain't my game."

"Aw, come on, Eddie. I'll get even on you!" Marty said.

"Ask Gelberg. It's his game," Eddie said, straightening

himself and shoving his chalk into his pants pocket. He trotted suddenly into the middle of the street and ran sideways a few feet. "Here go!" he hollered. "All the way!"

From his place up near the corner Paulie Dahler heaved the ball high into the air, higher than the telephone wires.

5   Marty bent his knees like a catcher, pounded his fist into his palm as though he were wearing a mitt, and held out his hands. "Here go, Eddie!" he hollered. "Here go!"

Holding the ball in his hand, and without answering him, Eddie walked toward the curb, where the rest of the fellows were gathered around Gelberg. Marty straightened his knees, put down his hands, and, sniffling his nose, trotted after Eddie.

6   "All right, I'll choose Gelberg for sides," Eddie said.

Gelberg heaved himself off the curb and put on his punchball glove, which was one of his mother's old kid gloves, with the fingers and thumb cut off short. "Odds, once takes it," he said.

After a couple of preparatory swings of their arms, they matched fingers. Gelberg won. He chose Albie Newbauer, Eddie looked around him and took Wally Reinhard. Gelberg took Ray-Ray Stickerling. Eddie took Wally Reinhard's brother Howey.

Marty hopped around on the edge of the group. "Hey, Gelberg," he hollered in a high voice. "Gimme a game, will you?"

7   "I got Arnie," Gelberg said.

Eddie looked around him again. "All right, I got Paulie Dahler."

They counted their men. "Choose you for up first," Gelberg said. Feeling as though he were going to cry, Marty watched them as they swung their arms, stuck out their fingers. This time Eddie won. Gelberg gathered his men around him and they trotted into the street to take up positions on the field. They hollered, "Here go!" threw the ball from first to second, then out into the field, and back again to Gelberg in the pitcher's box.

8   Marty ran over to him. "Gimme a game, will you, Gelberg?"

"We're all choosed up," Gelberg said, heaving a high one to Arnie out in center field.

Marty wiped his nose on his sleeve. "Come on, gimme a game. Didn't I let you lose my Spalding Hi-Bouncer down the sewer once?"

9   "Want to give the kid a game?" Gelberg called to Eddie, who was seated on the curb, figuring out his batting order with his men.

"Aw, we got the sides all choosed up!" Eddie said.

Marty stuck out his lower lip and wished that he would not have to cry. "You give Howey Reinhard a game!" he said, pointing at Howey sitting on the curb box next to Eddie. "He can't play any better than me!"

10   "Yeah," Howey yelled, swinging back his arm as though he were going to punch Marty in the jaw. "You couldn't hit the side of the house!"

"Yeah, I can play better than you any day!" Marty hollered.

"You can play left outside!" Howey said, looking around to see how the joke went over.

"Yeah, I'll get even on you!" Marty hollered, hoping that maybe they would get worried and give him a game after all.

11   With a fierce expression on his face, as if to indicate that he was through joking and now meant serious business, Howey sprang up from the curb and sent him staggering with a shove. Marty tried to duck, but Howey smacked him across the side of the head. Flinging his arms up about his ears, Marty scrambled down the street; for no reason at all Paulie Dahler booted him in the pants as he went by.

"I'll get even on you!" Marty yelled when he was out of reach. With a sudden movement of his legs, Howey pretended to rush at him. Almost falling over himself in panic, Marty dashed toward the house, but stopped, feeling ashamed, when he saw that Howey had only wanted to make him run.

12   For a while he stood there on the curb, wary and ready to dive into the house the instant any of the fellows made a move toward him. But presently he saw that the game was beginning, and that none of them was paying any more attention to him. He crept toward them again and, seating himself on the curb a little distance away, watched the game start. For a moment he thought of breaking it up, rushing up to the scoreboard and smudging it with his sneakers before anyone could stop him, and then dashing into the house before they caught him. Or grabbing the ball when it came near him and flinging it down the sewer. But he decided not to; the fellows would catch him in the end, smack him, and make

another scoreboard or get another ball, and then he would never get a game.

Every minute feeling more and more like crying, he sat there on the curb, his elbow on his knee, his chin in his palm, and tried to think where he could get another fellow, so that they could give him a game and still have even sides. Then he lifted his chin from his palm and saw that the new kid was sitting out on the stoop in front of the house, chewing something and gazing toward the game; and all at once the feeling that he was going to cry disappeared. He sprang up from the curb.

13 "Hey, Gelberg!" he hollered. "If I get the new kid for even sides, can I get a game?"

Without waiting for an answer, he dashed down the street toward the stoop where the new kid was sitting.

"Hey, fellow!" he shouted. "Want a game? Want a game of punchball?"

He could see now that what the new kid was eating was a slice of rye bread covered with applesauce. He could see too that the new kid was smaller than he was, and had a narrow face and a large nose with a few little freckles across the bridge. He was wearing Boy Scout pants and a brown woolen pullover, and on the back of his head was a skullcap made from the crown of a man's felt hat, the edge turned up and cut into sharp points that were ornamented with brass paper clips.

14 The new kid looked at him and took another bite of rye bread. "I don't know," he said, with his mouth full of bread, turning to take another look at the fellows in the street. "I guess I got to go to the store soon."

"You don't have to go to the store right away, do you?" Marty said in a high voice.

The new kid swallowed his bread and continued looking up toward the game. "I got to stay in front of the house in case my mother calls me."

"Maybe she won't call you for a while," Marty said. He could see that the inning was ending, that they would be starting a new inning in a minute, and his legs twitched with impatience.

"I don't know," the new kid said, still looking up at the game. "Anyway, I got my good shoes on."

15 "Aw, I bet you can't even play punchball!" cried Marty.

The new kid looked at him with his lower lip stuck out. "Yeah, I can so play! Only I got to go to the store!"

Once more he looked undecidedly up toward the game. Marty could see that the inning was over now. He turned pleadingly to the new kid.

"You can hear her if she calls you, can't you? Can't you play just till she calls you? Come on, can't you?"

Putting the last of his rye bread into his mouth, the new kid got up from the stoop. "Well, when she calls me," he said, brushing off the seat of his pants with his hand, "when she calls me I got to quit and go to the store."

16 As fast as he could run, Marty dashed up the street with the new kid trailing after him. "Hey, I got another man for even sides!" he yelled. "Gimme a game now? I got another man!"

The fellows looked at the new kid coming up the street behind Marty.

17 "You new on the block?" Howie Reinhard asked, eyeing the Boy Scout pants, as Marty and the new kid came up to them.

"You any good?" Gelberg demanded, bouncing the ball at his feet and looking at the skullcap ornamented with brass paper clips. "Can you hit?"

"Come on!" Marty said. He wished that they would just give him a game and not start asking a lot of questions. "I got another man for even sides, didn't I?"

"Aw, we got the game started already!" Ray-Ray Stickerling hollered.

18 Marty sniffled his nose, which was beginning to run again, and looked at him as fiercely as he was able. "It ain't your game!" he yelled. "It's Gelberg's game! Ain't it your game, Gelberg?"

Gelberg gave him a shove. "No one said you weren't going to get a game!" With a last bounce of his ball he turned to Eddie, who was looking the new kid over carefully.

"All right, Eddie. I'll take the new kid and you can have Marty."

19 Eddie drew his arm back as though he were going to hit him. "Like fun! Why don't you take Marty, if you're so wise?"

"I won the choose-up!" Gelberg hollered.

"Yeah, that was before! I'm not taking Marty!"

"I won the choose-up, didn't I?"

"Well, you got to choose up again for the new kid!"

Marty watched them as they stood up to each other, each eyeing the other suspiciously, and swung their arms to choose. Eddie won. "Cheating shows!" he yelled, seizing the new kid by the arm and pulling him into the group on his side.

20   Trying to look like the ballplayers he had seen the time his father had taken him to the Polo Grounds, Marty ran into the outfield and took the position near the curb that Gelberg had selected for him. He tried not to feel bad because Eddie had taken the new kid, that no one knew anything about, how he could hit, or anything; and that he had to go to the loser of the choose-up. As soon as he was out in the field he leaned forward, with his hands propped on his knees, and hollered: "All right, all right, these guys can't hit!" Then he straightened up and pounded his fist into his palm as though he were wearing a fielder's glove and shouted: "Serve it to them on a silver platter, Gelberg! These guys are just a bunch of fan artists!" He propped his hands on his knees again, like a big-leaguer, but all the while he felt unhappy, not nearly the way he should have felt, now that they had finally given him a game. He hoped that they would hit to him, and that he would make one-handed catches over his head, run way out with his back to the ball and spear them blind, or run in with all his might and pick them right off the tops of his shoes.

21   A little nervous chill ran through his back as he saw Paulie Dahler get up to hit. On Gelberg's second toss Paulie stepped in and sent the ball sailing into the air. A panic seized Marty as he saw it coming at him. He took a step nervously forward, then backward, then forward again, trying as hard as he could to judge the ball. It smacked into his cupped palms, bounced out, and dribbled toward the curb. He scrambled after it, hearing them shouting at him, and feeling himself getting more scared every instant. He kicked the ball with his sneaker, got his hand on it, and, straightening himself in a fever of fright, heaved it with all his strength at Ray-Ray on first. The moment the ball left his hand, he knew he had done the wrong thing. Paulie was already on his way to second; and besides, the throw was wild. Ray-Ray leaped into the air, his arms flung up, but it was way over his head, bouncing beyond him on the sidewalk and almost hitting a woman who was rocking a baby carriage at the door of the apartment house opposite.

With his heart beating the same way it did whenever anyone chased him, Marty watched Paulie gallop across the plate. He sniffled his nose, which was beginning to run again, and felt like crying.

22   "Holy Moses!" he heard Gelberg yell. "What do you want, a basket? Can't you hold on to them once in a while?"

"Aw, the sun was in my eyes!" Marty said.

"You wait until you want another game!" Gelberg shouted.

Breathing hard, Ray-Ray got back on first and tossed the ball to Gelberg. "Whose side are you on anyway?" he hollered.

Eddie Deakes put his hands to his mouth like a megaphone. "Attaboy, Marty!" he yelled. "Having you out there is like having another man on our side!"

The other fellows on the curb laughed, and Howey Reinhard made them laugh harder by pretending to catch a fly ball with the sun in his eyes, staggering around the street with his eyes screwed up and his hands cupped like a sissy, so that the wrists touched and the palms were widely separated.

23   No longer shouting or punching his fist into his palm, Marty took his place out in the field again. He stood there, feeling like crying, and wished that he hadn't dropped that ball or thrown it over Ray-Ray's head. Then, without knowing why, he looked up to see whether the new kid was laughing at him like all the rest. But the new kid was sitting a little off by himself at one end of the row of fellows on the curb, and with a serious expression on his face gnawed at the skin at the side of his thumbnail. Marty began to wonder if the new kid was any good or not. He saw him sitting there, with the serious look on his face, his ears sticking out, not joking like the other fellows, and from nowhere the thought leaped into Marty's head that maybe the new kid was no good. He looked at the skinny legs, the Boy Scout pants, and the mama's-boy shoes, and all at once he began to hope that Eddie would send the new kid in to hit, so that he could know right away whether he was any good or not.

24   But Wally Reinhard was up next. He fouled out on one of Gelberg's twirls, and after him Howey popped up to Albie Newbauer and Eddie was out on first. The fellows ran in to watch Eddie chalk up Paulie's run on the scoreboard alongside the sewer. They were still beefing and hollering at Marty for dropping that ball, but he pre-

tended he did not hear them and sat down on the curb to watch the new kid out in the field.

He was over near the curb, playing in closer than Paulie Dahler. Marty could see that he was not hollering "Here go!" or "All the way!" like the others, but merely stood there with that serious expression on his face and watched them throw the ball around. He held one leg bent at the ankle, so that the side of his shoe rested on the pavement, his belly was stuck out, and he chewed the skin at the side of his thumbnail.

Gelberg got up to bat. Standing in the pitcher's box, Eddie turned around and motioned his men to lay out. The new kid looked around him to see what the other fellows did, took a few steps backward, and then, with his belly stuck out again, went on chewing his thumb.

Marty felt his heart begin to beat hard. He watched Gelberg stand up to the plate and scornfully fling back the first few pitches.

"Come on, gimme one like I like!" Gelberg hollered.

"What's the matter! You afraid to reach for them?" Eddie yelled.

"Just pitch them to me, that's all!" Gelberg said.

Eddie lobbed one in that bounced shoulder high. With a little sideways skip Gelberg lammed into it.

25   The ball sailed down toward the new kid. Feeling his heart begin to beat harder, Marty saw him take a hurried step backward and at the same moment fling his hands before his face and duck his head. The ball landed beyond him and bounded up on the sidewalk. For an instant the new kid hesitated, then he was galloping after it, clattering across the pavement in his polished shoes.

Swinging his arms in mock haste, Gelberg breezed across the plate. "Get a basket!" he hollered over his shoulder. "Get a basket!"

26   Marty let his nose run without bothering to sniffle. He jumped up from the curb and curved his hands around his mouth like a megaphone. "He's scared of the ball!" he yelled at the top of his lungs. "He's scared of the ball! That's what he is, scared of the ball!"

The new kid tossed the ball back to Eddie. "I wasn't scared!" he said, moistening his lips with his tongue. "I wasn't scared! I just couldn't see it coming!"

27   With an expression of despair on his face, Eddie shook his head. "Holy Moses! If you can't see the ball,

why do you try to play punchball?" He bounced the ball hard at his feet and motioned Gelberg to send in his next batter. Arnie got up from the curb and, wiping his hands on his pants, walked toward the plate.

Marty felt his heart pounding in his chest. He hopped up and down with excitement and, seizing Gelberg by the arm, pointed at the new kid.

"You see him duck?" he yelled. "He's scared of the ball, that's what he is!" He hardly knew where to turn first. He rushed up to Ray-Ray, who was sitting on the curb making marks on the asphalt with the heel of his sneaker. "The new kid's scared to stop a ball! You see him duck!"

28   The new kid looked toward Marty and wet his lips with his tongue. "Yeah," he yelled, "didn't you muff one that was right in your hands?"

He was looking at Marty with a sore expression on his face, and his lower lip stuck out; and a sinking feeling went through Marty, a sudden sick feeling that maybe he had started something he would be sorry for. Behind him on the curb he could hear the fellows sniggering in that way they did when they picked on him. In the pitcher's box Eddie let out a loud cackling laugh.

29   "Yeah, the new kid's got your number!"

"The sun was in my eyes!" Marty said. He could feel his face getting red, and in the field the fellows were laughing. A wave of self-pity flowed through him.

"What are you picking on me for?" he yelled in a high voice. "The sun was so in my eyes. Anyway, I ain't no yellow-belly! I wasn't scared of the ball!"

The instant he said it he was sorry. He sniffled his nose uneasily as he saw Gelberg look at Ray-Ray. For an instant he thought of running into the house before anything happened. But instead he just stood there, sniffling his nose and feeling his heart beating, fast and heavy.

30   "You hear what he called you?" Paulie Dahler yelled at the new kid.

"You're not going to let him get away with calling you a yellow-belly, are you?" Eddie said, looking at the new kid.

The new kid wet his lips with his tongue and looked at Marty. "I wasn't scared!" he said. He shifted the soles of his new-looking shoes on the pavement. "I wasn't scared! I just couldn't see it coming, that's all!"

31   Eddie was walking toward the new kid now, bouncing

the ball slowly in front of him as he walked. In a sudden panic Marty looked back toward the house where Old Lady Kipnis lived. She always broke up fights; maybe she would break up this one; maybe she wouldn't even let it get started. But she wasn't out on her porch. He sniffled his nose, and with all his might hoped that the kid's mother would call him to go to the store.

"Any kid that lets himself be called a yellow-belly must be a yellow-belly!" Albie Newbauer said, looking around him for approval.

"Yeah," Gelberg said. "I wouldn't let anyone call me a yellow-belly."

32   With a sudden shove Eddie sent the new kid scrambling toward Marty. He tried to check himself by stiffening his body and twisting to one side, but it was no use. Before he could recover his balance, another shove made him stagger forward.

Marty sniffled his nose and looked at the kid's face close in front of him. It seemed as big as the faces he saw in the movies; and he could see that the kid's nose was beginning to run just like his own; and he could see in the corner of his mouth a crumb of the rye bread he had eaten on the stoop. For a moment the kid's eyes looked squarely into Marty's, so that he could see the little dark specks in the colored part around the pupil. Then the glance slipped away to one side; and all at once Marty had a feeling that the new kid was afraid of him.

33   "You gonna let him get away with calling you a yellow-belly?" he heard Eddie say. From the way it sounded he knew that the fellows were on his side now. He stuck out his jaw and waited for the kid to answer.

"I got to go to the store!" the new kid said. There was a scared look on his face and he took a step back from Marty.

Paulie Dahler got behind him and shoved him against Marty. Although he tried not to, Marty couldn't help flinging his arms up before his face. But the new kid only backed away and kept his arms at his sides. A fierce excitement went through Marty as he saw how scared the look on the kid's face was. He thrust his chest up against the new kid.

34   "Yellow-belly!" he hollered, making his voice sound tough. "Scared of the ball!"

The new kid backed nervously away, and there was a look on his face as though he wanted to cry.

"Yeah, he's scared!" Eddie yelled.

"Slam him, Marty!" Wally Reinhard hollered. "The kid's scared of you!"

"Aw, sock the yellow-belly!" Marty heard Gelberg say, and he smacked the kid as hard as he could on the shoulder. The kid screwed up his face to keep from crying and tried to back through the fellows ringing around him.

"Lemme alone!" he yelled.

35   Marty looked at him fiercely, with his jaw thrust forward, and felt his heart beating. He smacked the kid again, making him stagger against Arnie in back of him.

"Yeah, yellow-belly!" Marty hollered, feeling how the fellows were on his side and how scared the new kid was. He began smacking him again and again on the shoulder.

36   "Three, six, nine, a bottle of wine, I can fight you any old time!" he yelled. With each word he smacked the kid on the shoulder or arm. At the last word he swung with all his strength. He meant to hit the kid on the shoulder, but at the last instant, even while his arm was swinging, something compelled him to change his aim; his fist caught the kid on the mouth with a hard, wet socking sound. The shock of his knuckles against the kid's mouth, and that sound of it, made Marty want to hit him again and again. He put his head down and began swinging wildly, hitting the new kid without any aim on the head and shoulders and arms.

The new kid buried his head in his arms and began to cry. "Lemme alone!" he yelled. He tried to rush through the fellows crowded around him.

With all his might Marty smacked him on the side of the head. Rushing up behind him, Arnie smacked him too. Paulie Dahler shoved the skullcap, with its paper-clip ornaments, over the kid's eyes; and as he went by, Gelberg booted him in the pants.

37   Crying and clutching his cap, the new kid scampered over to the curb out of reach.

"I'll get even on you!" he cried.

With a fierce expression on his face Marty made a sudden movement of his legs and pretended to rush at him. The kid threw his arms about his head and darted down the street toward the house. When he saw that Marty was not coming after him, he sat down on the stoop; and Marty could see him rubbing his knuckles against his mouth.

Howey Reinhard was making fun of the new kid, scampering up and down the pavement with his arms wrapped around his head and hollering, "Lemme alone! Lemme alone!" The fellows laughed, and although he was breathing hard and his hand hurt from hitting the kid, Marty had to laugh too.

38 "You see him duck when that ball came at him?" he panted at Paulie Dahler.

Paulie shook his head. "Boy, just wait until we get the yellow-belly in the schoolyard!"

"And on Halloween," Gelberg said. "Wait until we get him on Halloween with our flour stockings!" He gave Marty a little shove and made as though he were whirling an imaginary flour stocking around his head.

39 Standing there in the middle of the street, Marty suddenly thought of Halloween, of the winter and snowballs, of the schoolyard. He saw himself whirling a flour stocking around his head and rushing at the new kid, who scampered in terror before him, hollering, "Lemme alone! Lemme alone!" As clearly as if it were in the movies, he saw himself flinging snowballs and the new kid backing into a corner of the schoolyard, with his hands over his face. Before he knew what he was doing, Marty turned fiercely toward the stoop where the new kid was still sitting, rubbing his mouth and crying.

40 "Hey, yellow-belly!" Marty hollered; and he pretended he was going to rush at the kid.

Almost falling over himself in fright, the new kid scrambled inside the house. Marty stood in the middle of the street and sniffled his nose. He shook his fist at the empty doorway.

"You see him run?" he yelled, so loud that it made his throat hurt. "Boy, you see him run?" He stood there shaking his fist, although the new kid was no longer there to see him. He could hardly wait for the winter, for Halloween, or the very next day in the schoolyard.

Discussion

1. From whose point of view do you witness the incidents described in "The New Kid"? Do you know what any of the boys in the story are thinking? If so, does knowing what each is thinking make a difference in how you feel

toward him? Toward the other boys? Explain your answer.

2. Who is saying the sentences inside the parentheses in paragraph 1? How do you know? What do those sentences tell you about the speaker? About Marty?

3. What information in passages 1 through 4 tells you something about Marty's age and suggests that he is not accepted by the other boys? How old do you think Marty is? Why?

4. As you read passages 8 through 12, how did you feel about Marty? About the other boys? Do you see things from Marty's point of view in those passages? Why? Do the other kids see from Marty's point of view? Explain your answer.

5. You meet "the new kid" in passages 13 through 15. What is your impression of him? What does he do and say to give you that impression? How is his relationship to Marty similar to, or different from, Marty's relationship to the other boys?

6. What technique does Marty use to get "the new kid" to play? What does this tell you about Marty?

7. How does Marty act after the choose-up? Why? Do you think his actions represent his true feelings? If not, what are his true feelings?

8. When and how do you find out why the boys did not want Marty to play? Does this information make their point of view more understandable? Why or why not?

9. Why does Marty make a fuss about "the new kid's" being "scared of the ball"? How does "the new kid" react? How do the other boys react?

10. When Marty thinks that "the new kid" might be afraid of him, how does this change Marty's view of himself? How does this affect Marty's relationship with the other boys?

11. As "the new kid" went by, "Gelberg booted him in the pants." Why is that action significant? Has this happened before? When? To whom?

12. From the time that Gelberg boots "the new kid," is Marty's point of view toward "the new kid" different? How? Why? How does Marty's relationship with the other boys change?

Writing Assignment 1

Rewrite a part of the story from "the new kid's" point of view. You may want to start your story with Marty's asking "the new kid" if he wants to play.

Put yourself in "the new kid's" shoes. What does he see? What does he think? How does he react to Marty's invitation? To Eddie? To Gelberg and the others?

Do not simply recount everything that happens from the time Marty asks "the new kid" to play. Rather, tell only those things that would be significant to "the new kid" from his point of view.

Will "the new kid" remain nameless in your story? Why? Will all the other boys have names if you tell the story from his point of view? If they do not have names, how will you have "the new kid" identify them?

Writing Assignment 2

Select any part of "The New Kid" you can retell from the point of view of one of the boys besides Marty and "the new kid." What does he see? What does he think? How does he react?

Do not try to retell the entire story: rather, select one incident that you can recount from a totally new point of view. Will you have the boy you choose say more than he does in the original story? Will your reader discover more of your character's thoughts than he did as he read the original story? Why? How?

Before you begin to write, reread "The New Kid," paying particular attention to the actions and speech of the character you have selected; study him carefully so you can project his actions and thoughts during the incident.

Writing Assignment 3

Write a story in which the central character is a person who has a real or imaginary handicap. For example, the person may be the smallest kid in the class, or the biggest. He or she may be afraid of the dark or afraid of heights. Or your character may have some kind of physical handicap. But before you choose the handicap, be sure you understand it well enough to know how a person with such a handicap would react in a variety of situations.

After you have decided who your central character is and what his handicap will be, start jotting down information you will need. The following questions may help you:

1. What does my character look like? What descriptive details does my reader need to get a sharp mental picture of my character?
2. How old is the central character? Is it necessary for the reader to know how old he is so that the reader will have a better idea of why the person behaves in a certain manner?
3. Is the character's handicap physical or emotional? What effect does the handicap have on the character's view of himself? What effect does it have on the way others view him? What effect does it have on the way he reacts to them?

After you have a good idea of what your character looks like, how he thinks, and how he reacts toward others, you will want to begin thinking about a problem that the person must solve or a situation in which he must act. The following questions may help you create a situation:

1. Given a specific handicap, what situation can I put my character into that will force him either to overcome his handicap or be defeated by it? Or do I want my character to succeed in solving a problem because of his handicap? As I think of situations, do I know enough about them to describe them adequately? Do I know enough about them to have my character act or react realistically?
2. If the situation or problem involves other characters, who are they? What do they look like? Are they sympathetic to my central character, or are they antagonistic? Why? Who evokes the sympathy or provokes the antagonism?
3. What distinct characteristics does each minor character have? What effect do these characteristics have on the problem or situation?

It will probably be best for you to tell the story from the point of view of the central character.

Having chosen the central character, the handicap, the minor characters, and the situation or problem, you may now begin the actual writing of the story.

As you develop it, you may find the following questions useful:

1. What does the central character do to control the situation or solve the problem? Does he succeed or fail? Why? Will the reader, relying on the information I give, understand the motives of the central character—that is, will the reader understand why my character thinks and acts as he does?
2. Am I developing the central character realistically? Am I giving the reader enough information through description or through the character's thoughts and/or actions for the reader to understand why my character behaves and thinks as he does?
3. Do I have the characters talk in the story? Do they say things that "real" people would say? Will my reader think that the dialogue is realistic or will he call it phony? Why?
4. How does the story end? Why do I have it end that way? Is the ending—the central character's success or failure in getting out of the situation or solving the problem—believable? Why, or why not?

Chapter 4

Never Having
Been Here Before,
I Can't Say

"How do you like our fair city?" the lady asked.

"I don't know," the man said. "Never having been here before, I can't say."

Have you ever been asked a question about a new face, a new place, or a new experience that you couldn't answer? Have you ever been afraid to go someplace and do something because it would be a new experience and you didn't know what to expect? Have you ever said things during a new experience that didn't make too much sense; you just said them because you thought you had to say something?

"How do you like our fair city now?" the lady asked.

"It sure does have a lot of tall buildings," the man replied.

If you have ever responded to a question in that manner, you might have wondered why when you thought about it later. But at the time, the excitement of a new situation might prompt you to blurt out something that you might think is foolish later. Perhaps all the man could think about was the tall buildings. And perhaps all you could think about on your first day of school was chewing gum, as Jim Davy does in the following story:

The First Day of School
by William Saroyan

1   He was a little boy named Jim, the first and only child of Dr. Louis Davy, 717 Mattei Building, and it was his first day at school. His father was French, a small heavy-

set man of forty whose boyhood had been full of poverty and unhappiness and ambition. His mother was dead: she died when Jim was born, and the only woman he knew intimately was Amy, the Swedish housekeeper.

It was Amy who dressed him in his Sunday clothes and took him to school. Jim liked Amy, but he didn't like for her taking him to school. He told her so. All the way to school he told her so.

2 I don't like you, he said. I don't like you any more.

I like *you,* the housekeeper said.

Then why are you taking me to school? he said.

He had taken walks with Amy before, once all the way to the Court House Park for the Sunday afternoon band concert, but this walk to school was different.

3 What for? he said.

Everybody must go to school, the housekeeper said.

Did you go to school? he said.

No, said Amy.

Then why do I have to go? he said.

You will like it, said the housekeeper.

4 He walked on with her in silence, holding her hand. I don't like you, he said. I don't like you any more.

I like you, said Amy.

Then why are you taking me to school? he said again. Why?

5 The housekeeper knew how frightened a little boy could be about going to school.

You will like it, she said. I think you will sing songs and play games.

I don't want to, he said.

I will come and get you every afternoon, she said.

I don't like you, he told her again.

She felt very unhappy about the little boy going to school, but she knew that he would have to go.

6 The school building was very ugly to her and to the boy. She didn't like the way it made her feel, and going up the steps with him she wished he didn't have to go to school. The halls and rooms scared her, and him, and the smell of the place, too. And he didn't like Mr. Barber, the principal.

Amy despised Mr. Barber.

7 What is the name of your son? Mr. Barber said.

This is Dr. Louis Davy's son, said Amy. His name is Jim. I am Dr. Davy's housekeeper.

James? said Mr. Barber.

Not James, said Amy, just Jim.

All right, said Mr. Barber. Any middle name?

No, said Amy. He is too small for a middle name. Just Jim Davy.

8   All right, said Mr. Barber. We'll try him out in the first grade. If he doesn't get along all right, we'll try him out in kindergarten.

Dr. Davy said to start him in the first grade, said Amy. Not kindergarten.

All right, said Mr. Barber.

9   The housekeeper knew how frightened the little boy was, sitting on the chair, and she tried to let him know how much she loved him and how sorry she was about everything. She wanted to say something fine to him about everything, but she couldn't say anything, and she was very proud of the nice way he got down from the chair and stood beside Mr. Barber, waiting to go with him to a classroom.

On the way home she was so proud of him she began to cry.

10   Miss Binney, the teacher of the first grade, was an old lady who was all dried out. The room was full of little boys and girls. School smelled strange and sad. He sat at a desk and listened carefully.

He heard some of the names: *Charles, Ernest, Alvin, Norman, Betty, Hannah, Juliet, Viola, Polly.*

11   He listened carefully and heard Miss Binney say, Hannah Winter, what *are* you chewing? And he saw Hannah Winter blush. He liked Hannah Winter right from the beginning.

Gum, said Hannah.

Put it in the wastebasket, said Miss Binney.

He saw the little girl walk to the front of the class, take the gum from her mouth, and drop it in the wastebasket.

12   And he heard Miss Binney say, Ernest Gaskin, what are *you* chewing?

Gum, said Ernest.

And he liked Ernest Gaskin, too.

They met in the schoolyard, and Ernest taught him a few jokes.

13   Amy was in the hall when school ended. She was sullen and angry at everybody until she saw the little

boy. She was amazed that he wasn't changed, that he wasn't hurt, or perhaps utterly unalive, murdered. The school and everything about it frightened her very much. She took his hand and walked out of the building with him, feeling angry and proud.

14   Jim said, What comes after twenty-nine?

Thirty, said Amy.

Your face is dirty, he said.

His father was very quiet at the supper table.

What comes after twenty-nine? the boy said.

Thirty, said his father.

Your face is dirty, he said.

15   In the morning he asked his father for a nickel.

What do you want a nickel for? his father said.

Gum, he said.

His father gave him a nickel, and on the way to school he stopped at Mrs. Riley's store and bought a package of spearmint.

16   Do you want a piece? he asked Amy.

Do you want to give me a piece? the housekeeper said.

Jim thought about it a moment, and then he said, Yes.

Do you like me? said the housekeeper.

I like you, said Jim. Do you like me?

Yes, said the housekeeper. Do you like school?

Jim didn't know for sure, but he knew he liked the part about gum. And Hannah Winter. And Ernest Gaskin.

I don't know, he said.

Do you sing? asked the housekeeper.

No, we don't sing, he said.

Do you play games? she said.

Not in the school, he said. In the yard we do.

He liked the part about gum very much.

17   Miss Binney said, Jim Davy, what are you *chewing?*

Ha ha ha, he thought.

Gum, he said.

He walked to the wastepaper basket and back to his seat, and Hannah Winter saw him, and Ernest Gaskin too. That was the best part of school.

It began to grow, too.

18   Ernest Gaskin, he shouted in the schoolyard, *what* are you *chewing?*

Raw elephant meat, said Ernest Gaskin. Jim Davy, what are *you* chewing?

Jim tried to think of something very funny to be chewing, but he couldn't.

Gum, he said, and Ernest Gaskin laughed louder than Jim laughed when Ernest Gaskin said raw elephant meat.

It was funny no matter what you said.

Going back to the classroom, Jim saw Hannah Winter in the hall.

19   Hannah Winter, he said, *what in the world* are you *chewing?*

The little girl was startled. She wanted to say something nice that would honestly show how nice she felt about having Jim say her name and ask her the funny question, making fun of school, but she couldn't think of anything that nice to say because they were almost in the room and there wasn't time enough.

Tutti-frutti, she said with desperate haste.

It seemed to Jim he had never before heard such a glorious word, and he kept repeating the word to himself all day.

20   Tutti-frutti, he said to Amy on the way home.

Amy Larson he said, *what, are, you, chewing?*

He told his father all about it at the supper table.

He said, Once there was a hill. On the hill there was a mill. Under the mill there was a walk. Under the walk there was a key. What is it?

I don't know, his father said. What is it?

Milwaukee, said the boy.

The housekeeper was delighted.

Mill. Walk. Key, Jim said.

Tutti-frutti.

What's that? said his father.

Gum, he said. The kind Hannah Winter chews.

Who's Hannah Winter? said his father.

She's in my room, he said.

Oh, said his father.

21   After supper he sat on the floor with the small red and blue and yellow top that hummed while it spinned. It was all right, he guessed. It was still very sad, but the gum part of it was very funny and the Hannah Winter part very nice. Raw elephant meat, he thought with great inward delight.

Raw elephant meat, he said aloud to his father who was reading the evening paper. His father folded the paper and sat on the floor beside him. The housekeeper saw them together on the floor, and for some reason tears came to her eyes.

Discussion

1. What does the first paragraph tell you about Jim that helps you understand his initial reaction to going to school? How does this information make you feel about him?
2. Why does Jim blame Amy for his having to go to school? If he were older, would he still blame her? What would an older person know that Jim doesn't?
3. What is your first impression of Amy? Is there a difference between what she says to Jim about school and what she thinks? How does this make you feel toward her? Do you like her more or less because of it? Does Amy seem to know more about how Jim feels than he knows about how she feels? Explain.
4. The first paragraph of passage 10 describes the teacher as "an old lady who was all dried out," and tells you that "school smelled strange and sad." Is it clear who is describing the teacher and the school? Does it make a difference? How and why? Do you think the narrator was being intentionally vague? What effect does this passage have on you? Why?
5. Why do you think the author chose gum chewing as a focus for the story? Why does Jim like Hannah and Ernest before he even knows them? Does he understand what is happening when they have to deposit their gum in the wastebasket? Why or why not? Why does he like "the part about gum" so much?
6. When Amy returns to get Jim after his first day of school, what are her feelings? What are his? What has happened to Jim during his first day to change his attitude toward school? What is his new attitude?
7. Why is Jim so pleased when he gets to take his gum to the wastebasket? How do you feel about him in passage 17? Does he understand what is happening? Do you? Do the rest of the kids? Is it important for Jim to know what is happening? Does the teacher realize how Jim is interpreting the whole gum chewing business? How and why do their points of view differ?
8. In passage 20 Jim tells his father "all about it" at the supper table. What is "it"? Why does Jim think "tutti-frutti" is such a "glorious" word?

9. In passage 21, why does "raw elephant meat" give Jim "great inward delight"? When he says it aloud to his father, does his father understand what it means? Explain your answer.
10. What did Jim learn in school?

Writing Assignment 1

Recall your own past and select an incident in which you (or some other child—sister, brother, friend, acquaintance) did not really understand what was happening to you or what was going on around you. If you are like the rest of us, there are many such incidents for you to pick from. Write about the incident from a child's point of view, indicating by your rendering of the child's thoughts, feelings, words, and actions how he or she is interpreting and reacting to the situation.

The following incident may help you as you prepare to write. One Sunday morning the three-year-old daughter of one of the writers of this book attended church with her mother. She had been going to church regularly for about a year. This particular morning mother and daughter were a little early, and after waiting for several minutes for the service to begin, the little girl asked her mother in a very loud voice, "When is God going to get here?" From the point of view of her mother and the people sitting around them, the question was very funny. However, it suggests all kinds of interesting things that older people never really think about. As the incident is briefly related here, we can only guess what the child was thinking. If you were to try to relate this story from her point of view, you would need to ask questions such as: What does church mean to a three-year-old child? What do the things that go on there mean to her? Who does she think God is? What is she thinking as she sits there? What have all of her previous visits to church meant to her? How does she fit this into her other experiences? Such questions and their answers can help you to think about the things that you understand and take for granted but that are completely mysterious to a child, or have been interpreted by him in what may seem to you very unusual ways.

The following questions, which were actually asked by a child, may be helpful to you as you prepare to write your own story. They are not intended to be a basis for your assignment; they are only meant to illustrate what questions one particular child asked.

Where do birthdays come from?
What do you do when you sleep?
What is a trick or treat?
Who cooks God's supper?
Why can't a little girl *marry* her father?
How come the moon follows us outside but never comes in the house?

As you prepare to write, you might want to ask yourself the following questions:

1. What has the child said or done that indicates something about what he is thinking? What might be going on in his mind, and how can I convey that in written language?
2. Why do I see the event differently than he does? What experiences have given me information and a perspective that the child could not possibly have? Which parts of my own experiences do I have to ignore in order to think as the child is likely to?
3. What language do I use to make it sound like a young child? Do I have to use "baby talk," or can I convey a child's thoughts with "adult language"? How?

Remember your task is to see and think as a child might; you are to convey the experience from the child's point of view, not explain why the child is thinking as he does. What you must do here, actually, is forget what your experience has taught you instead of learning from it and being influenced by it.

NEW EXPERIENCES

Children face new experiences every day. When you think of the many new, chaotic, perhaps even frightening experiences children must face every day during their first few years of life, you can't help but be amazed at their ability to interpret and understand what they encounter.

Of course, the older we get the fewer completely new situations we face; our previous experiences help us to accumulate a savings account of knowledge upon which we can draw when we do encounter unfamiliar situations. The greater the number and variety of our past experiences, the larger the resources we have to draw upon. Because of this, people have been prompted to say and believe that there is really nothing new in this world. Even though that may be partially true, the fact is that each individual must learn and experience for himself. The experiences of his mother and father cannot be passed along to him like the color of his skin, hair, and eyes. Newness is relative and individual.

The problem of adapting to new experiences is not solved, however, merely by growing up. Even though new experiences become rarer, it seems that when we do encounter a new one, it becomes increasingly difficult to adapt as we grow older. Maybe past experience has more than one effect upon us: it can make us better able to understand a new experience, but it may also make us form habits that leave us less able to adapt to, or even to recognize, what is new, different, or unusual.

Whatever the case, it is obvious that experience or lack of it is one of the most significant influences upon our point of view. The experiences we bring from the past help us to interpret or misinterpret the present. Sometimes our past experience just doesn't prepare us for some experiences, or our past experiences may cause us to act in peculiar ways and never even question the reason for our actions. The following stories show how experience may influence actions, not always in predictable ways.

I Sing the Body Electric!
by Ray Bradbury

1   Grandma!

   I remember her birth.

   What, you say, *no* man remembers his own grandma's birth.

   But, yes, *we* remember the day that she was born.

   For we, her grandchildren, slapped her to life. Timothy, Agatha, and I, Tom, raised up our hands and brought them down in a huge crack! We shook together the bits and pieces, parts and samples, textures and tastes, humors and distillations that would move her compass needle north to cool us, south to warm and comfort us, east and west to travel round the endless world, glide her eyes to know us, mouth to sing us asleep by night, hands to touch us awake at dawn.

Grandma, O dear and wondrous electric dream . . .

When storm lightnings rove the sky making circuitries amidst the clouds, her name flashes on my inner lid. Sometimes still I hear her ticking, humming above our beds in the gentle dark. She passes like a clock-ghost in the long halls of memory, like a hive of intellectual bees swarming after the Spirit of Summers Lost. Sometimes still I feel the smile I learned from her, printed on my cheek at three in the deep morn . . .

All right, all right! you cry, what was it like the day your damned and wondrous-dreadful-loving Grandma was born?

It was the week the world ended . . .

Our mother was dead.

One late afternoon a black car left Father and the three of us stranded on our own front drive staring at the grass, thinking:

2   That's not our grass. There are the croquet mallets, balls, hoops, yes, just as they fell and lay three days ago when Dad stumbled out on the lawn, weeping with the news. There are the roller skates that belonged to a boy, me, who will never be that young again. And yes, there was the tire-swing on the old oak, but Agatha afraid to swing. It would surely break. It would fall.

3   And the house? Oh, God . . .

We peered through the front door, afraid of the echoes we might find confused in the halls; the sort of clamor that happens when all the furniture is taken out and there is nothing to soften the river of talk that flows in any house at all hours. And now the soft, the warm, the main piece of lovely furniture was gone forever.

The door drifted wide.

Silence came out. Somewhere a cellar door stood wide and a raw wind blew damp earth from under the house.

But, I thought, we don't *have* a cellar!

"Well," said Father.

We did not move.

Aunt Clara drove up the path in her big canary-colored limousine.

We jumped through the door. We ran to our rooms.

4   We heard them shout and then speak and then shout and then speak: Let the children live with me! Aunt Clara said. They'd rather kill themselves! Father said.

A door slammed. Aunt Clara was gone.

We almost danced. Then we remembered what had happened and went downstairs.

Father sat alone talking to himself or to a remnant ghost of Mother left from the days before her illness, but jarred loose now by the slamming of the door. He murmured to his hands, his empty palms:

"The children need someone. I love them but, let's face it, I must work to feed us all. You love them, Ann, but you're gone. And Clara? Impossible. She loves but smothers. And as for maids, nurses—?"

Here Father sighed and we sighed with him, remembering.

The luck we had had with maids or live-in teachers or sitters was beyond intolerable. Hardly a one who wasn't a crosscut saw grabbing against the grain. Hand-axes and hurricanes best described them. Or, conversely, they were all fallen trifle, damp soufflé. We children were unseen furniture to be sat upon or dusted or sent for re-upholstering come spring and fall, with a yearly cleansing at the beach.

5   "What we need," said Father, "is a . . ."

We all leaned to his whisper.

". . . grandmother."

"But," said Timothy, with the logic of nine years, "all our grandmothers are dead."

"Yes in one way, no in another."

What a fine mysterious thing for Dad to say.

"Here," he said at last.

He handed us a multifold, multicolored pamphlet. We had seen it in his hands, off and on, for many weeks, and very often during the last few days. Now, with one blink of our eyes, as we passed the paper from hand to hand, we knew why Aunt Clara, insulted, outraged, had stormed from the house.

Timothy was the first to read aloud from what he saw on the first page:

"I Sing the Body Electric!"

He glanced up at Father, squinting. "What the heck does that mean?"

"Read on."

Agatha and I glanced guiltily about the room, afraid

Mother might suddenly come in to find us with this blasphemy, but then nodded to Timothy, who read:

" 'Fanto—' "

"Fantoccini," Father prompted.

" 'Fantoccini Ltd. *We Shadow Forth* ... the answer to all your most grievous problems. One Model Only, upon which a thousand times a thousand variations can be added, subtracted, subdivided, indivisible, with Liberty and Justice for all.' "

"Where does it say *that?*" we all cried.

"It doesn't." Timothy smiled for the first time in days. "I just had to put that in. Wait." He read on: " 'for you who have worried over inattentive sitters, nurses who cannot be trusted with marked liquor bottles, and well-meaning Uncles and Aunts—' "

"Well-meaning, *but!*" said Agatha, and I gave an echo.

" '—we have perfected the first humanoid-genre mini-circuited, rechargeable AC-DC Mark V Electrical Grandmother ...' "

"Grandmother!?"

The paper slipped away to the floor. "Dad ... ?"

"Don't look at me that way," said Father. "I'm half-mad with grief, and half-mad thinking of tomorrow and the day after that. Someone pick up the paper. Finish it."

"I will," I said, and did:

6   " 'The Toy that is more than a Toy, the Fantoccini Electrical Grandmother is built with loving precision to give the incredible precision of love to your children. The child at ease with the realities of the world and the even greater realities of the imagination, is her aim.

" 'She is computerized to tutor in twelve languages simultaneously, capable of switching tongues in a thousandth of a second without pause, and has a complete knowledge of the religious, artistic, and sociopolitical histories of the world seeded in her master hive—' "

"How great!" said Timothy. "It makes it sound as if we were to keep bees! *Educated* bees!"

"Shut up!" said Agatha.

" 'Above all,' " I read, " 'this human being, for human she seems, this embodiment in electro-intelligent facsimile of the humanities, will listen, know, tell, react and love your children insofar as such great Objects, such fantastic Toys, can be said to Love, or can be imagined to Care. This Miraculous Companion, excited to the challenge of large world and small, inner Sea or Outer Universe, will transmit by touch and tell, said Miracles to your Needy.' "

"Our Needy," murmured Agatha.

Why, we all thought, sadly, that's us, oh, yes, that's *us*.

I finished:

" 'We do not sell our Creation to able-bodied families where parents are available to raise, effect, shape, change, love their own children. Nothing can replace the parent in the home. However, there are families where death or ill health or disablement undermines the welfare of the children. Orphanages seem not the answer. Nurses tend to be selfish, neglectful, or suffering from dire nervous afflictions.

" 'With the utmost humility then, and recognizing the need to rebuild, rethink, and regrow our conceptualizations from month to month, year to year, we offer the nearest thing to the Ideal Teacher-Friend-Companion-Blood Relation. A trial period can be arranged for—' "

7   "Stop," said Father. "Don't go on. Even *I* can't stand it."

I folded the pamphlet up. "Do they *really* have these things?"

"Let's not talk any more about it," said Father, his hand over his eyes. "It was a mad thought—"

"Not so mad," I said, glancing at Tim. "I mean, heck, even if they tried, whatever they built, couldn't be worse than Aunt Clara, huh?"

And then we all roared. We hadn't laughed in months. And now my simple words made everyone hoot and howl and explode. I opened my mouth and yelled happily, too.

When we stopped laughing, we looked at the pamphlet and I said, "Well?"

"I—" Agatha scowled, not ready.

"We do need something, bad, right now," said Timothy.

"I have an open mind," I said, in my best pontifical style.

"There's only one thing," said Agatha. "We can try it. Sure.

"But—tell me this—when do we cut out all this talk and when does our *real* mother come home to stay?"

There was a single gasp from the family as if, with one shot, she had struck us all in the heart.

I don't think any of us stopped crying the rest of that night.

8   It was a clear bright day. The helicopter tossed us lightly up and over and down through the skyscrapers and let us out, almost for a trot and caper, on top of the building where the large letters could be read from the sky:
FANTOCCINI.
"What are *Fantoccini?*" said Agatha.
"It's an Italian word for shadow puppets, I think, or dream people," said Father.
"But *shadow forth,* what does that mean?"
"WE TRY TO GUESS YOUR DREAM," I said.
"Bravo," said Father. "A-Plus."
I beamed.
The helicopter flapped a lot of loud shadows over us and went away.
We sank down in an elevator as our stomachs sank up. We stepped out onto a moving carpet that streamed away on a blue river of wool toward a desk over which various signs hung:

THE CLOCK SHOP
Fantoccini Our Specialty
Rabbits on walls, no problem.

"Rabbits on walls?"
I held up my fingers in profile as if I held them before a candle flame, and wiggled the "ears."
"Here's a rabbit, here's a wolf, here's a crocodile."
"Of course," said Agatha.
And we were at the desk. Quiet music drifted about us. Somewhere behind the walls, there was a waterfall of machinery flowing softly. As we arrived at the desk, the lighting changed to make us look warmer, happier, though we were still cold.
All about us in niches and cases, and hung from ceilings on wires and strings were puppets and marionettes, and Balinese kite-bamboo-translucent dolls which, held to the moonlight, might acrobat your most secret nightmares or dreams. In passing, the breeze set up by our bodies stirred the various hung souls on their gibbets. It was like an immense lynching on a holiday at some English crossroads four hundred years before.
You see? I know my history.

9   Agatha blinked about with disbelief and then some touch of awe and finally disgust.

"Well, if that's what they are, let's go."

"Tush," said Father.

"Well," she protested, "you gave me one of those dumb things with strings two years ago and the strings were in a zillion knots by dinnertime. I threw the whole thing out the window."

"Patience," said Father.

10   "We shall see what we can do to eliminate the strings."

The man behind the desk had spoken.

We all turned to give him our regard.

Rather like a funeral-parlor man, he had the cleverness not to smile. Children are put off by older people who smile too much. They smell a catch, right off.

Unsmiling, but not gloomy or pontifical, the man said, "Guido Fantoccini, at your service. Here's how we do it, Miss Agatha Simmons, aged eleven."

Now there was a really fine touch.

He knew that Agatha was only ten. Add a year to that, and you're halfway home. Agatha grew an inch. The man went on:

"There."

And he placed a golden key in Agatha's hand.

"To wind them up instead of strings?"

"To wind them up." The man nodded.

"Pshaw!" said Agatha.

Which was her polite form of "rabbit pellets."

"God's truth. Here is the key to your Do-it-Yourself, Select Only the Best, Electrical Grandmother. Every morning you wind her up. Every night you let her run down. You're in charge. You are guardian of the Key."

He pressed the object in her palm where she looked at it suspiciously.

I watched him. He gave me a side wink which said, well, no . . . but aren't keys fun?

I winked back before she lifted her head.

"Where does this fit?"

"You'll see when the time comes. In the middle of her stomach, perhaps, or up her left nostril or in her right ear."

That was good for a smile as the man arose.

"This way, please. Step light. Onto the moving stream. Walk on the water, please. Yes. There."

He helped to float us. We stepped from rug that was forever frozen onto rug that whispered by.

It was a most agreeable river which floated us along on a green spread of carpeting that rolled forever through halls and into wonderfully secret dim caverns where voices echoed back our own breathing or sang like Oracles to our questions.

"Listen," said the salesman, "the voices of all kinds of women. Weigh and find just the right one . . . !"

And listen we did, to all the high, low, soft, loud, in-between, half-scolding, half-affectionate voices saved over from times before we were born.

And behind us, Agatha trod backward, always fighting the river, never catching up, never with us, holding off.

"Speak," said the salesman. "Yell."

And speak and yell we did.

"Hello. You there! This is Timothy, hi!"

"What shall I say!" I shouted. "Help!"

Agatha walked backward, mouth tight.

Father took her hand. She cried out.

"Let go! No, no! I won't have my voice used! I won't!"

"Excellent." The salesman touched three dials on a small machine he held in his hand.

On the side of the small machine we saw three oscillograph patterns mix, blend, and repeat our cries.

11   The salesman touched another dial and we heard our voices fly off amidst the Delphic caves to hang upside down, to cluster, to beat words all about, to shriek, and the salesman itched another knob to add, perhaps, a touch of this or a pinch of that, a breath of mother's voice, all unbeknownst, or a splice of father's outrage at the morning's paper or his peaceable one-drink voice at dusk. Whatever it was the salesman did, whispers danced all about us like frantic vinegar gnats, fizzed by lightning, settling round until at last a final switch was pushed and a voice spoke free of a far electronic deep:

"Nefertiti," it said.

Timothy froze. I froze. Agatha stopped treading water.

"Nefertiti?" asked Tim.

"What does that mean?" demanded Agatha.

"I know."

The salesman nodded me to tell.

"Nefertiti," I whispered, "is Egyptian for The Beautiful One Is Here."

"The Beautiful One Is Here," repeated Timothy.

"Nefer," said Agatha, "titi."

And we all turned to stare into that soft twilight, that deep far place from which the good warm soft voice came.

And she was indeed there.

And, by her voice, she was beautiful . . .

12 That was it.

That was, at least, the most of it.

The voice seemed more important than all the rest.

Not that we didn't argue about weights and measures:

She should not be bony to cut us to the quick, nor so fat we might sink out of sight when she squeezed us.

Her hand pressed to ours, or brushing our brow in the middle of sick-fever nights, must not be marble-cold, dreadful, or oven-hot, oppressive, but somewhere between. The nice temperature of a baby-chick held in the hand after a long night's sleep and just plucked from beneath a contemplative hen; that, that was it.

Oh, we were great ones for detail. We fought and argued and cried, and Timothy won on the color of her eyes, for reasons to be known later.

Grandmother's hair? Agatha, with girl's ideas, though reluctantly given, she was in charge of that. We let her choose from a thousand harp strands hung in filamentary tapestries like varieties of rain we ran amongst. Agatha did not run happily, but seeing we boys would mess things in tangles, she told us to move aside.

And so the bargain shopping through the dimestore inventories and the Tiffany extensions of the Ben Franklin Electric Storm Machine and Fantoccini Pantomime Company was done.

And the always flowing river ran its tide to an end and deposited us all on a far shore in the late day.

13 It was very clever of the Fantoccini people, after that.

How?

They made us wait.

They knew we were not won over. Not completely, no, nor half completely.

Especially Agatha, who turned her face to her wall and saw sorrow there and put her hand out again and again to touch it. We found her fingernail marks on the wallpaper each morning, in strange little silhouettes, half beauty, half nightmare. Some could be erased with a breath, like ice flowers on a winter pane. Some could not be rubbed out with a washcloth, no matter how hard you tried.

14 And meanwhile, they made us wait.

So we fretted out June.

So we sat around July.

So we groused through August and then on August 29, "I have this feeling," said Timothy, and we all went out after breakfast to sit on the lawn.

Perhaps we had smelled something on Father's conversation the previous night, or caught some special furtive glance at the sky or the freeway Rapped briefly and then lost in his gaze. Or perhaps it was merely the way the wind blew the ghost curtains out over our beds, making pale messages all night.

For suddenly there we were in the middle of the grass, Timothy and I, with Agatha, pretending no curiosity, up on the porch, hidden behind the potted geraniums.

We gave her no notice. We knew that if we acknowledged her presence, she would flee, so we sat and watched the sky where nothing moved but birds and highflown jets, and watched the freeway where a thousand cars might suddenly deliver forth our Special Gift . . . but . . . nothing.

At noon we chewed grass and lay low . . .

At one o'clock, Timothy blinked his eyes.

And then, with incredible precision, it happened.

It was as if the Fantoccini people knew our surface tension.

All children are water-striders. We skate along the top skin of the pond each day, always threatening to break through, sink, vanish beyond recall, into ourselves.

Well, as if knowing our long wait must absolutely end within one minute! this *second!* no more, God, forget it!

At that instant, I repeat, the clouds above our house opened wide and let forth a helicopter like Apollo driving his chariot across mythological skies.

15 And the Apollo machine swam down on its own summer breeze, wafting hot winds to cool, reweaving our hair, smartening our eyebrows, applauding our pant legs against our shins, making a flag of Agatha's hair on the

porch and thus settled like a vast frenzied hibiscus on our lawn, the helicopter slid wide a bottom drawer and deposited upon the grass a parcel of largish size, no sooner having laid same then the vehicle, with not so much as a god bless or farewell, sank straight up, disturbed the calm air with a mad ten thousand flourishes and then, like a skyborne dervish, tilted and fell off to be mad some other place.

16   Timothy and I stood riven for a long moment looking at the packing case, and then we saw the crowbar taped to the top of the raw pine lid and seized it and began to pry and creak and squeal the boards off, one by one, and as we did this I saw Agatha sneak up to watch and I thought thank you, God, thank you that Agatha never saw a coffin, when Mother went away, no box, no cemetery, no earth, just words in a big church, no box, no box like *this* . . . !

The last pine plank fell away.

Timothy and I gasped. Agatha, between us now, gasped, too.

For inside the immense raw pine package was the most beautiful idea anyone ever dreamt and built.

Inside was the perfect gift for any child from seven to seventy-seven.

We stopped up our breaths. We let them out in cries of delight and adoration.

Inside the opened box was . . .

A mummy.

Or, first anyway, a mummy case, a sarcophagus!

"Oh, no!" Happy tears filled Timothy's eyes.

"It can't be!" said Agatha.

"It is, it is!"

"Our very own?"

"Ours!"

"It must be a mistake!"

"Sure, they'll want it back!"

"They can't *have* it!"

"Lord, Lord, is that real gold!? Real hieroglyphs! Run your fingers over them!"

"Let *me!*"

"Just like in the museums! Museums!"

We all grabbed at once. I think some tears fell from my own eyes to rain upon the case.

"Oh, they'll make the colors run!"

Agatha wiped the rain away.

17   And the golden mask face of the woman carved on the sarcophagus lid looked back at us with just the merest smile which hinted at our own joy, which accepted the overwhelming upsurge of a love we thought had drowned forever but now surfaced into the sun.

Not only did she have a sun-metal face stamped and beaten out of purest gold, with delicate nostrils and a mouth that was both firm and gentle, but her eyes, fixed into their sockets, were cerulean or amethystine or lapus lazuli, or all three, minted and fused together, and her body was covered over with lions and eyes and ravens, and her hands were crossed upon her carved bosom and in one gold mitten she clenched a thonged whip for obedience, and in the other a fantastic ranuncula, which makes for obedience out of love, so the whip lies unused . . .

18   And as our eyes ran down her hieroglyphs it came to all three of us at the same instant:

"Why, those signs!" "Yes, the hen tracks!" "The birds, the snakes!"

They didn't speak tales of the Past.

They were hieroglyphs of the Future.

This was the first queen mummy delivered forth in all time whose papyrus inkings etched out the next month, the next season, the next year, the next *lifetime!*

She did not mourn for time spent.

No. She celebrated the bright coinage yet to come, banked, waiting, ready to be drawn upon and used.

We sank to our knees to worship that possible time.

19   First one hand, then another, probed out to niggle, twitch, touch, itch over the signs.

"There's me, yes, look! Me, in sixth grade!" said Agatha, now in the fifth. "See the girl with my-colored hair and wearing my gingerbread suit?"

"There's me in the twelfth year of high school!" said Timothy, so very young now but building taller stilts every week and stalking around the yard.

"There's me," I said, quietly, warm, "in college. The guy wearing glasses who runs a little to fat. Sure. Heck." I snorted. "That's me."

The sarcophagus spelled winters ahead, springs to squander, autumns to spend with all the golden and rusty and copper leaves like coins, and over all, her bright sun symbol, daughter-of-Ra eternal face, forever above our horizon, forever an illumination to tilt our shadows to better ends.

20   "Hey!" we all said at once, having read and reread our Fortune-Told scribblings, seeing our lifelines and lovelines, inadmissible, serpentined over, around, and down. "Hey!"

And in one séance table-lifting feat, not telling each other what to do, just doing it, we pried up the bright sarcophagus lid, which had no hinges but lifted out like cup from cup, and put the lid aside.

And within the sarcophagus, of course, was the true mummy!

And she was like the image carved on the lid, but more so, more beautiful, more touching because human shaped, and shrouded all in new fresh bandages of linen, round and round, instead of old and dusty cerements.

And upon her hidden face was an identical golden mask, younger than the first, but somehow, strangely wiser than the first.

And the linens that tethered her limbs had symbols on them of three sorts, one a girl of ten, one a boy of nine, and a boy of thirteen.

A series of bandages for each of us!

We gave each other a startled glance and a sudden bark of laughter.

Nobody said the bad joke, but all thought:

She's all wrapped up in us!

And we didn't care. We loved the joke. We loved whoever had thought to make us part of the ceremony we now went through as each of us seized and began to unwind each of his or her particular serpentines of delicious stuffs!

21   The lawn was soon a mountain of linen.

The woman beneath the covering lay there, waiting.

"Oh, no," cried Agatha. "She's dead, too!"

She ran. I stopped her. "Idiot. She's not dead *or* alive. Where's your key?"

"Key?"

"Dummy," said Tim, "the key the man gave you to wind her up!"

Her hand had already spidered along her blouse to where the symbol of some possible new religion hung. She had strung it there, against her own skeptic's muttering, and now she held it in her sweaty palm.

22   "Go on," said Timothy. "Put it in!"

"But *where?*"

"Oh for God's sake! As the man said, in her right armpit or left ear. Gimme!"

And he grabbed the key and impulsively moaning with impatience and not able to find the proper insertion slot, prowled over the prone figure's head and bosom and at last, on pure instinct, perhaps for a lark, perhaps just giving up the whole damned mess, thrust the key through a final shroud of bandage at the navel.

On the instant: *spunnng!*

The Electrical Grandmother's eyes flicked wide!

Something began to hum and whir. It was as if Tim had stirred up a hive of hornets with an ornery stick.

"Oh," gasped Agatha, seeing he had taken the game away, "let *me!*"

She wrenched the key.

Grandma's nostrils *flared!* She might snort up steam, snuff out fire!

"Me!" I cried, and grabbed the key and gave it a huge . . . *twist!*

The beautiful woman's mouth popped wide.

"Me!"

"Me!"

"Me!"

Grandma suddenly sat up.

We leapt back.

We knew we had, in a way, slapped her alive.

She was born, she was *born!*

Her head swiveled all about. She gaped. She mouthed. And the first thing she said was:

Laughter.

Where one moment we had backed off, now the mad sound drew us near to peer as in a pit where crazy folk are kept with snakes to make them well.

23   It was a good laugh, full and rich and hearty, and it did not mock, it accepted. It said the world was a wild place, strange, unbelievable, absurd if you wished, but all in all, quite a place. She would not dream to find another. She would not ask to go back to sleep.

She was awake now. We had awakened her. With a glad shout, she would go with it all.

And go she did, out of her sarcophagus, out of her winding sheet, stepping forth, brushing off, looking around as for a mirror. She found it.

The reflections in our eyes.

She was more pleased than disconcerted with what she found there. Her laughter faded to an amused smile.

24   For Agatha, at the instant of birth, had leapt to hide on the porch.

The Electrical Person pretended not to notice.

She turned slowly on the green lawn near the shady street, gazing all about with new eyes, her nostrils moving as if she breathed the actual air and this the first morn of the lovely Garden and she with no intention of spoiling the game by biting the apple . . .

Her gaze fixed upon my brother.

"You must be—?"

"Timothy. Tim," he offered.

"And you must be—?"

"Tom," I said.

How clever again of the Fantoccini Company. *They* knew. *She* knew. But they had taught her to pretend not to know. That way we could feel great, we were the teachers, telling her what she already knew! How sly, how wise.

"And isn't there another boy?" said the woman.

"Girl!" a disgusted voice cried from somewhere on the porch.

"Whose name is Alicia—?"

"Agatha!" The far voice, started in humiliation, ended in proper anger.

"Algernon, of course."

"Agatha!" Our sister popped up, popped back to hide a flushed face.

"Agatha." The woman touched the word with proper affection. "Well, Agatha, Timothy, Thomas, let me *look* at you."

"No," said I, said Tim, "Let us look at *you*. Hey . . ."

Our voices slid back in our throats.

We drew near her.

25   We walked in great slow circles round about, skirting the edges of her territory. And her territory extended as far as we could hear the hum of the warm summer hive. For that is exactly what she sounded like. That was her characteristic tune. She made a sound like a season all to herself, a morning early in June when the world wakes to find everything absolutely perfect, fine, delicately attuned, all in balance, nothing disproportioned. Even before you opened your eyes you knew it would be one of those days.

Tell the sky what color it must be, and it was indeed. Tell the sun how to crochet its way, pick and choose among leaves to lay out carpetings of bright and dark on the fresh lawn, and pick and lay it did. The bees have been up earliest of all, they have already come and gone, and come and gone again to the meadow fields and returned all golden fuzz on the air, all pollen-decorated, epaulettes at the full, nectar-dripping. Don't you hear them pass? hover? dance their language? telling where all the sweet gums are, the syrups that make bears frolic and lumber in bulked ecstasies, that make boys squirm with unpronounced juices, that make girls leap out of beds to catch from the corners of their eyes their dolphin selves naked aflash on the warm air poised forever in one eternal glass wave.

So it seemed with our electrical friend here on the new lawn in the middle of a special day.

And she a stuff to which we were drawn, lured, spelled, doing our dance, remembering what could not be remembered, needful, aware of her attentions.

Timothy and I, Tom, that is.

Agatha remained on the porch.

But her head flowered above the rail, her eyes followed all that was done and said.

26 And what was said and done was Tim at last exhaling:

"Hey . . . your *eyes* . . ."

Her eyes. Her splendid eyes.

Even more splendid than the lapis lazuli on the sarcophagus lid and on the mask that had covered her bandaged face. These most beautiful eyes in the world looked out upon us calmly, shining.

"Your eyes," gasped Tim, "are the *exact* same color, are like—"

"Like what?"

"My favorite aggies . . ."

"What could be better than that?" she said.

And the answer was, nothing.

27 Her eyes slid along on the bright air to brush my ears, my nose, my chin. "And you, Master Tom?"

"Me?"

"How shall we be friends? We must, you know, if we're going to knock elbows about the house the next year . . ."

"I . . ." I said, and stopped.

"You," said Grandma, "are a dog mad to bark but with taffy in his teeth. Have you ever given a dog taffy? It's so sad and funny, both. You laugh but hate yourself for laughing. You cry and run to help, and laugh again when his first new bark comes out."

I barked a small laugh remembering a dog, a day, and some taffy.

Grandma turned, and there was my old kite strewn on the lawn. She recognized its problem.

"The string's broken. No. The ball of string's *lost*. You can't fly a kite that way. Here."

She bent. We didn't know what might happen. How could a robot grandma fly a kite for us? She raised up, the kite in her hands.

"Fly," she said, as to a bird.

And the kite flew.

That is to say, with a grand flourish, she let it up on the wind.

And she and the kite were one.

For from the tip of her index finger there sprang a thin bright strand of spider web, all half-invisible gossamer fishline which, fixed to the kite, let it soar a hundred, no, three hundred, no, a thousand feet high on the summer swoons.

Timothy shouted. Agatha, torn between coming and going, let out a cry from the porch. And I, in all my maturity of thirteen years, though I tried not to look impressed, grew taller, taller, and felt a similar cry burst out my lungs, and burst it did. I gabbled and yelled lots of things about how I wished *I* had a finger from which, on a bobbin, I might thread the sky, the clouds, a wild kite all in one.

"If you think *that* is high," said the Electric Creature, "watch *this!*"

With a hiss, a whistle, a hum, the fishline sung out. The kite sank up another thousand feet. And again another thousand, until at last it was a speck of red confetti dancing on the very winds that took jets around the world or changed the weather in the next existence . . .

"It can't be!" I cried.

"It *is*." She calmly watched her finger unravel its massive stuffs. "I make it as I need it. Liquid inside, like a spider. Hardens when it hits the air, instant thread . . ."

And when the kite was no more than a specule, a vanishing mote on the peripheral vision of the gods, to quote from older wisemen, why then Grandma, without turning, without looking, without letting her gaze offend by touching, said:

28   "And, Abigail—?"

"Agatha!" was the sharp response.

O wise woman, to overcome with swift small angers.

"Agatha," said Grandma, not too tenderly, not too lightly, somewhere poised between, "and how shall *we* make do?"

She broke the thread and wrapped it about my fist three times so I was tethered to heaven by the longest, I repeat, longest kite string in the entire history of the world! Wait till I show my friends! I thought. Green! Sour apple green is the color they'll turn!

"Agatha?"

"No way!" said Agatha.

"No way," said an echo.

"There must be some—"

"We'll never be friends!" said Agatha.

"Never be friends," said the echo.

Timothy and I jerked. Where was the echo coming from? Even Agatha, surprised, showed her eyebrows above the porch rail.

Then we looked and saw.

Grandma was cupping her hands like a seashell and from within that shell the echo sounded.

"Nèver . . . friends . . ."

And again faintly dying "Friends . . ."

We all bent to hear.

That is we two boys bent to hear.

"No!" cried Agatha.

And ran in the house and slammed the doors.

"Friends," said the echo from the seashell hands. "No."

And far away, on the shore of some inner sea, we heard a small door shut.

And that was the first day.

29   And there was a second day, of course, and a third and a fourth, with Grandma wheeling in a great circle, and we her planets turning about the central light, with Agatha slowly, slowly coming in to join, to walk if not run with us, to listen if not hear, to watch if not see, to itch if not touch.

But at least by the end of the first ten days, Agatha

no longer fled, but stood in nearby doors, or sat in distant chairs under trees, or if we went out for hikes, followed ten paces behind.

And Grandma? She merely waited. She never tried to urge or force. She went about her cooking and baking apricot pies and left foods carelessly here and there about the house on mousetrap plates for wiggle-nosed girls to sniff and snitch. An hour later, the plates were empty, the buns or cakes gone and without thank you's, there was Agatha sliding down the banister, a mustache of crumbs on her lip.

As for Tim and me, we were always being called up hills by our Electric Grandma, and reaching the top were called down the other side.

30 And the most peculiar and beautiful and strange and lovely thing was the way she seemed to give complete attention to all of us.

She listened, she really listened to all we said, she knew and remembered every syllable, word, sentence, punctuation, thought, and rambunctious idea. We knew that all our days were stored in her, and that any time we felt we might want to know what we said at X hour at X second on X afternoon, we just named that X and with amiable promptitude, in the form of an aria if we wished, sung with humor, she would deliver forth X incident.

31 Sometimes we were prompted to test her. In the midst of babbling one day with high fevers about nothing, I stopped. I fixed Grandma with my eye and demanded:

"What did I just say?"

"Oh, er—"

"Come on, spit it out!"

"I think—" she rummaged her purse. "I have it here." From the deeps of her purse she drew forth and handed me:

"Boy! A Chinese fortune cookie!"

"Fresh baked, still warm, open it."

It was almost too hot to touch. I broke the cookie shell and pressed the warm curl of paper out to read:

"—bicycle Champ of the whole West! What did I just say? Come on, spit it out!"

My jaw dropped.

"How did you *do* that?"

"We have our little secrets. The only Chinese fortune cookie that predicts the Immediate Past. Have another?"

I cracked the second shell and read:

" 'How did you *do* that?' "

I popped the messages and the piping hot shells into my mouth and chewed as we walked.

"Well?"

"You're a great cook," I said.

And, laughing, we began to run.

And that was another great thing.

She could *keep up*.

Never beat, never win a race, but pump right along in good style, which a boy doesn't mind. A girl ahead of him or beside him is too much to bear. But a girl one or two paces back is a respectful thing, and allowed.

So Grandma and I had some great runs, me in the lead, and both talking a mile a minute.

32   But now I must tell you the best part of Grandma.

I might not have known at all if Timothy hadn't taken some pictures, and if I hadn't taken some also, and then compared.

When I saw the photographs developed out of our instant Brownies, I sent Agatha, against her wishes, to photograph Grandma a third time, unawares.

Then I took the three sets of pictures off alone, to keep counsel with myself. I never told Timothy and Agatha what I found. I didn't want to spoil it.

33   But, as I laid the pictures out in my room, here is what I thought and said:

"Grandma, in each picture, looks *different!*"

"Different?" I asked myself.

"Sure. Wait. Just a sec—"

I rearranged the photos.

"Here's one of Grandma near Agatha. And, in it, Grandma looks like . . . Agatha!

"And in this one, posed with Timothy, she looks like Timothy!

"And this last one, Holy Goll! Jogging along with me, she looks like ugly *me!*"

34   I sat down, stunned. The pictures fell to the floor.

I hunched over, scrabbling them, rearranging, turning upside down and sidewise. Yes. Holy Goll again, yes!

O that clever Grandmother.

O those Fantoccini people-making people.

Clever beyond clever, human beyond human, warm beyond warm, love beyond love . . .

And wordless, I rose and went downstairs and found Agatha and Grandma in the same room, doing algebra lessons in an almost peaceful communion. At least there was not outright war. Grandma was still waiting for Agatha to come round. And no one knew what day of what year that would be, or how to make it come faster. Meanwhile—

35   My entering the room made Grandma turn. I watched her face slowly as it recognized me. And wasn't there the merest ink-wash change of color in those eyes? Didn't the thin film of blood beneath the translucent skin, or whatever liquid they put to pulse and beat in the humanoid forms, didn't it flourish itself suddenly bright in her cheeks and mouth? I am somewhat ruddy. Didn't Grandma suffuse herself more to my color upon my arrival? And her eyes? Watching Agatha-Abigail-Algernon at work, hadn't they been *her* color of blue rather than mine, which are deeper?

More important than that, in the moments as she talked with me, saying, "Good evening," and "How's your homework, my lad?" and such stuff, didn't the bones of her face shift subtly beneath the flesh to assume some fresh racial attitude?

36   For let's face it, our family is of three sorts. Agatha has the long horse bones of a small English girl who will grow to hunt foxes; Father's equine stare, snort, stomp, and assemblage of skeleton. The skull and teeth are pure English, or as pure as the motley isle's history allows.

Timothy is something else, a touch of Italian from mother's side a generation back. Her family name was Mariano, so Tim has that dark thing firing him, and a small bone structure, and eyes that will one day burn ladies to the ground.

As for me, I am the Slav, and we can only figure this from my paternal grandfather's mother who came from Vienna and brought a set of cheekbones that flared, and temples from which you might dip wine, and a kind of steppeland thrust of nose which sniffed more of Tartar than of Tartan, hiding behind the family name.

So you see it became fascinating for me to watch and try to catch Grandma as she performed her changes, speaking to Agatha and melting her cheekbones to the horse, speaking to Timothy and growing as delicate as a Florentine raven pecking glibly at the air, speaking to me and fusing the hidden plastic stuffs, so I felt Catherine the Great stood there before me.

37   Now, how the Fantoccini people achieved this rare

and subtle transformation I shall never know, nor ask, nor wish to find out. Enough that in each quiet motion, turning here, bending there, affixing her gaze, her secret segments, sections, the abutment of her nose, the sculptured chinbone, the wax-tallow plastic metal forever warmed and was forever susceptible of loving change. Hers was a mask that was all mask but only one face for one person at a time. So in crossing a room, having touched one child, on the way, beneath the skin, the wondrous shift went on, and by the time she reached the next child, why, true mother of *that* child she was! looking upon him or her out of the battlements of their own fine bones.

And when *all* three of us were present and chattering at the same time? Well, then, the changes were miraculously soft, small, and mysterious. Nothing so tremendous as to be caught and noted, save by this older boy, myself, who, watching, became elated and admiring and entranced.

38   I have never wished to be behind the magician's scenes. Enough that the illusion works. Enough that love is the chemical result. Enough that cheeks are rubbed to happy color, eyes sparked to illumination, arms opened to accept and softly bind and hold . . .

All of us, that is, except Agatha who refused to the bitter last.

"Agamemnon . . ."

39   It had become a jovial game now. Even Agatha didn't mind, but pretended to mind. It gave her a pleasant sense of superiority over a supposedly superior machine.

"Agamemnon!" she snorted, "you *are* a d . . ."

"Dumb?" said Grandma.

"I wouldn't say that."

"Think it, then, my dear Agonistes Agatha . . . I am quite flawed, and on names my flaws are revealed. Tom there, is Tim half the time. Timothy is Tobias or Timulty as likely as not . . ."

40   Agatha laughed. Which made Grandma make one of her rare mistakes. She put out her hand to give my sister the merest pat. Agatha-Abigail-Alice leapt to her feet.

Agatha-Agamemnon-Alcibiades-Allegra-Alexandra-Allison withdrew swiftly to her room.

41   "I suspect," said Timothy, later, "because she is beginning to like Grandma."

"Tosh," said I.

"Where do you pick up words like Tosh?"

"Grandma read me some Dickens last night. 'Tosh.' 'Humbug.' 'Balderdash.' 'Blast.' 'Devil take you.' You're pretty smart for your age, Tim."

42 "Smart, heck. It's obvious, the more Agatha likes Grandma, the more she hates herself for liking her, the more afraid she gets of the whole mess, the more she hates Grandma in the end."

"Can one love someone so much you hate them?"

"Dumb. Of course."

"It *is* sticking your neck out, sure. I guess you hate people when they make you feel naked, I mean sort of on the spot or out in the open. That's the way to play the game, of course. I mean, you don't just love people you must LOVE them with exclamation points."

"You're pretty smart, yourself, for someone so stupid," said Tim.

"Many thanks."

And I went to watch Grandma move slowly back into her battle of wits and stratagems with what's-her-name . . .

43 What dinners there were at our house!

Dinners, heck; what lunches, what breakfasts!

Always something new, yet, wisely, it looked or seemed old and familiar. We were never asked, for if you ask children what they want, they do not know, and if you tell what's to be delivered, they reject delivery. All parents know this. It is a quiet war that must be won each day. And Grandma knew how to win without looking triumphant.

44 "Here's Mystery Breakfast Number Nine," she would say, placing it down. "Perfectly dreadful, not worth bothering with, it made me want to throw up while I was cooking it!"

Even while wondering how a robot could be sick, we could hardly wait to shovel it down.

"Here's Abominable Lunch Number Seventy-seven," she announced. "Made from plastic food bags, parsley, and gum from under theatre seats. Brush your teeth after or you'll taste the poison all afternoon."

We fought each other for more.

Even Abigail-Agamemnon-Agatha drew near and circled round the table at such times, while Father put on the ten pounds he needed and pinkened out his cheeks.

45   When A. A. Agatha did not come to meals, they were left by her door with a skull and crossbones on a small flag stuck in a baked apple. One minute the tray was abandoned, the next minute gone.

Other times Abigail A. Agatha would bird through during dinner, snatch crumbs from her plate and bird off.

"Agatha!" Father would cry.

"No, wait," Grandma said, quietly. "She'll come, she'll sit. It's a matter of time."

"What's wrong with her?" I asked.

"Yeah, for cri-yi, she's nuts," said Timothy.

"No, she's afraid," said Grandma.

"Of you?" I said, blinking.

"Not of me so much as what I might *do*," she said.

"You wouldn't do anything to hurt her."

"No, but she thinks I might. We must wait for her to find that her fears have no foundation. If I fail, well, I will send myself to the showers and rust quietly."

There was a titter of laughter. Agatha was hiding in the hall.

46   Grandma finished serving everyone and then sat at the other side of the table facing Father and pretended to eat. I never found out, I never asked, I never wanted to know, what she did with the food. She was a sorcerer. It simply vanished.

And in the vanishing, Father made comment:

"This food. I've had it before. In a small French restaurant over near Les Deux Magots in Paris, twenty, oh, twenty-five years ago!" His eyes brimmed with tears, suddenly.

"How do you *do* it?" he asked, at last, putting down the cutlery, and looking across the table at this remarkable creature, this device, this what? *woman?*

Grandma took his regard, and ours, and held them simply in her now empty hands, as gifts, and just as gently replied:

47   "I am given things which I then give to you. I don't *know* that I give, but the giving goes on. You ask what I am? Why, a machine. But even in that answer we know, don't we, more than a machine. I am all the people who thought of me and planned me and built me and set me running. So I am people. I am all the things they wanted to be and perhaps could not be, so they built a great child, a wondrous toy to represent those things."

48   "Strange," said Father. "When I was growing up,

there was a huge outcry at machines. Machines were bad, evil, they might dehumanize—"

"Some machines do. It's all in the way they are built. It's all in the way they are used. A bear trap is a simple machine that catches and holds and tears. A rifle is a machine that wounds and kills. Well, I am no bear trap. I am no rifle. I am a grandmother machine, which means more than a machine."

49   "How can you be more than what you seem?"

"No man is as big as his own idea. It follows, then, that any machine that embodies an idea is larger than the man that made it. And what's so wrong with that?"

"I got lost back there about a mile," said Timothy. "Come again?"

"Oh, dear," said Grandma. "How I do hate philosophical discussions and excursions into esthetics. Let me put it this way. Men throw huge shadows on the lawn, don't they? Then, all their lives, they try to run to fit the shadows. But the shadows are always longer. Only at noon can a man fit his own shoes, his own best suit, for a few brief minutes. But now we're in a new age where we can think up a Big Idea and run it around in a machine. That makes the machine more than a machine, doesn't it?"

"So far so good," said Tim. "I guess."

"Well, isn't a motion-picture camera and projector more than a machine? It's a thing that dreams, isn't it? Sometimes fine happy dreams, sometimes nightmares. But to call it a machine and dismiss it is ridiculous."

"I see *that!*" said Tim, and laughed at seeing.

50   "You must have been invented then," said Father, "by someone who loved machines and hated people who *said* all machines were bad or evil."

"Exactly," said Grandma. "Guido Fantoccini, that was his real name, grew up among machines. And he couldn't stand the clichés any more."

"Clichés?"

"Those lies, yes, that people tell and pretend they are truths absolute. Man will never fly. That was a cliché truth for a thousand thousand years which turned out to be a lie only a few years ago. The earth is flat, you'll fall off the rim, dragons will dine on you; the great lie told as fact, and Columbus plowed it under. Well, now, how many times have you heard how inhuman machines are, in your life? How many bright fine people have you heard spouting the same tired truths which are in reality lies; all machines destroy, all machines are cold, thoughtless, awful.

51   "There's a seed of truth there. But only a seed. Guido Fantoccini knew that. And knowing it, like most men of his kind, made him mad. And he could have stayed mad and gone mad forever, but instead did what he had to do; he began to invent machines to give the lie to the ancient lying truth.

52   "He knew that most machines are amoral, neither bad nor good. But by the way you built and shaped them you in turn shaped men, women, and children to be bad or good. A car, for instance, dead brute, unthinking, an unprogrammed bulk, is the greatest destroyer of souls in history. It makes boy-men greedy for power, destruction, and more destruction. It was never *intended* to do that. But that's how it turned out."

53   Grandma circled the table, refilling our glasses with clear cold mineral spring water from the tappet in her left forefinger. "Meanwhile, you must use other compensating machines. Machines that throw shadows on the earth' that beckon you to run out and fit that wondrous casting-forth. Machines that trim your soul in silhouette like a vast pair of beautiful shears, snipping away the rude brambles, the dire horns and hooves to leave a finer profile. And for that you need examples."

"Examples?" I asked.

"Other people who behave well, and you imitate them. And if you act well enough long enough all the hair drops off and you're no longer a wicked ape."

Grandma sat again.

54   "So, for thousands of years, you humans have needed kings, priests, philosophers, fine examples to look up to and say, 'They are good, I wish I could be like them. They set the grand good style.' But, being human, the finest priests, the tenderest philosophers make mistakes, fall from grace, and mankind is disillusioned and adopts indifferent skepticism or, worse, motionless cynicism and the good world grinds to a halt while evil moves on with huge strides."

55   "And you, why, you never make mistakes, you're perfect, you're better than anyone *ever!*"

It was a voice from the hall between kitchen and dining room where Agatha, we all knew, stood against the wall listening and now burst forth.

Grandma didn't even turn in the direction of the voice, but went on calmly addressing her remarks to the family at the table.

56   "Not perfect, no, for what is perfection? But this I do know: being mechanical, I cannot sin, cannot be bribed, cannot be greedy or jealous or mean or small. I do not relish power for power's sake. Speed does not pull me to madness. Sex does not run me rampant through the world. I have time and more than time to collect the information I need around and about an ideal to keep it clean and whole and intact. Name the value you wish, tell me the Ideal you want and I can see and collect and remember the good that will benefit you all. Tell me how you would like to be: kind, loving, considerate, well-balanced, humane . . . and let me run ahead on the path to explore those ways to be just that. In the darkness ahead, turn me as a lamp in all directions. I *can* guide your feet."

57   "So," said Father, putting the napkin to his mouth, "on the days when all of us are busy making lies—"

"I'll tell the truth."

"On the days when we hate—"

"I'll go on giving love, which means attention, which means knowing all about you, all, all, all about you, and you knowing that I know but that most of it I will never tell to anyone, it will stay a warm secret between us, so you will never fear my complete knowledge."

And here Grandma was busy clearing the table, circling, taking the plates, studying each face as she passed, touching Timothy's cheek, my shoulder with her free hand flowing along, her voice a quiet river of certainty bedded in our needful house and lives.

58   "But," said Father, stopping her, looking her right in the face. He gathered his breath. His face shadowed. At last he let it out. "All this talk of love and attention and stuff. Good God, woman, you, you're not *in* there!"

He gestured to her head, her face, her eyes, the hidden sensory cells behind the eyes, the miniaturized storage vaults and minimal keeps.

"*You're* not *in* there!"

Grandmother waited one, two, three silent beats.

Then she replied: "No. But *you* are. You and Thomas and Timothy and Agatha.

59   "Everything you ever say, everything you ever do, I'll keep, put away, treasure. I shall be all the things a

family forgets it is, but senses, half-remembers. Better than the old family albums you used to leaf through, saying here's this winter, there's that spring, I shall recall what you forget. And though the debate may run another hundred thousand years: What is Love? perhaps we may find that love is the ability of someone to give us back to us. Maybe love is someone seeing and remembering handing us back to ourselves just a trifle better than we had dared to hope or dream ...

"I am family memory and, one day perhaps, racial memory, too, but in the round, and at your call. I do not *know* myself. I can neither touch nor taste nor feel on any level. Yet I exist. And my existence means the heightening of your chance to touch and taste and feel. Isn't love in there somewhere in such an exchange? Well ..."

60   She went on around the table, clearing away, sorting and stacking, neither grossly humble nor arthritic with pride.

"What do I know?

"This, above all: the trouble with most families with many children is someone gets lost. There isn't time, it seems, for everyone. Well, I will give equally to all of you. I will share out my knowledge and attention with everyone. I wish to be a great warm pie fresh from the oven, with equal shares to be taken by all. No one will starve. Look! someone cries, and I'll look. Listen! someone cries, and I hear. Run with me on the river path! someone says, and I run. And at dusk I am not tired, nor irritable, so I do not scold out of some tired irritability. My eye stays clear, my voice strong, my hand firm, my attention constant."

61   "But," said Father, his voice fading, half convinced, but putting up a last faint argument, "you're not *there*. As for love—"

"If paying attention is love, I am love.

"If knowing is love, I am love.

"If helping you not to fall into error and to be good is love, I am love.

"And again, to repeat, there are four of you. Each, in a way never possible before in history, will get my complete attention. No matter if you all speak at once, I can channel and hear this one and that and the other, clearly. No one will go hungry. I will, if you please, and accept the strange word, 'love' you all."

62   "I *don't* accept!" said Agatha.

And even Grandma turned now to see her standing in the door.

"I won't give you permission, you can't, you mustn't!" said Agatha. "I won't let you! It's lies! You lie. No one loves me. She said she did, but she lied. She *said* but *lied!*"

"Agatha!" cried Father, standing up.

"She?" said Grandma. "Who?"

"Mother!" came the shriek. "Said: Love you! Lies! Love you! Lies! And you're like her! You lie. But you're empty, anyway, and so that's a *double* lie! I hate *her*. Now, I hate *you!*"

Agatha spun about and leapt down the hall.

The front door slammed wide.

63   Father was in motion, but Grandma touched his arm. "Let me."

And she walked and then moved swiftly, gliding down the hall and then suddenly, easily, running, yes, running very fast, out the door.

It was a champion sprint by the time we all reached the lawn, the sidewalk, yelling.

Blind, Agatha made the curb, wheeling about, seeing us close, all of us yelling, Grandma way ahead, shouting, too, and Agatha off the curb and out in the street, halfway to the middle, then the middle and suddenly a car, which no one saw, erupting its brakes, its horn shrieking and Agatha flailing about to see and Grandma there with her and hurling her aside and down as the car with fantastic energy and verve selected her from our midst, struck out wonderful electric Guido Fantoccini-produced dream even while she paced upon the air and, hands up to ward off, almost in mild protest, still trying to decide what to say to this bestial machine, over and over she spun and down and away even as the car jolted to a halt and I saw Agatha safe beyond and Grandma, it seemed, still coming down and sliding fifty yards away to strike and ricochet and lie strewn and all of us frozen in a line suddenly in the midst of the street with one scream pulled out of all our throats at the same raw instant.

Then silence and just Agatha lying on the asphalt, intact, getting ready to sob.

64   And still we did not move, frozen on the sill of death, afraid to venture in any direction, afraid to go see what

lay beyond the car and Agatha and so we began to wail and, I guess, pray to ourselves as Father stood amongst us: Oh, no, no, we mourned, oh no, God, no, no . . .

65   Agatha lifted her already grief-stricken face and it was the face of someone who has predicted dooms and lived to see and now did not want to see or live any more. As we watched, she turned her gaze to the tossed woman's body and tears fell from her eyes. She shut them and covered them and lay back down forever to weep . . .

I took a step and then another step and then five quick steps and by the time I reached my sister her head was buried deep and her sobs came up out of a place so far down in her I was afraid I could never find her again, she would never come out, no matter how I pried or pleaded or promised or threatened or just plain said. And what little we could hear from Agatha buried there in her own misery, she said over and over again, lamenting, wounded, certain of the old threat known and named and now here forever. ". . . like I said . . . told you . . . lies . . . lies . . . liars . . . all lies . . . like the other . . . other . . . just like . . . just . . . just like the other . . . other . . . other . . . !"

66   I was down on my knees holding onto her with both hands, trying to put her back together even though she wasn't broken any way you could see but just feel, because I knew it was no use going on to Grandma, no use at all, so I just touched Agatha and gentled her and wept while Father came up and stood over and knelt down with me and it was like a prayer meeting in the middle of the street and lucky no more cars coming, and I said, choking, "Other what, Ag, other *what?*"

67   Agatha exploded two words.

"Other dead!"

"You mean Mom?"

"O Mom," she wailed, shivering, lying down, cuddling up like a baby. "O Mom, dead, O Mom and now Grandma dead, she promised always, always, to love, to love, promised to be different, promised, promised and now look, look . . . I hate her, I hate Mom, I hate her, I hate *them!*"

68   "Of course," said a voice. "It's only natural. How foolish of me not to have known, not to have seen."

And the voice was so familiar we were all stricken.

We all jerked.

Agatha squinched her eyes, flicked them wide, blinked, and jerked half up, staring.

"How silly of me," said Grandma, standing there at the edge of our circle, our prayer, our wake.

"Grandma!" we all said.

And she stood there, taller by far than any of us in this moment of kneeling and holding and crying out. We could only stare up at her in disbelief.

69   "You're dead!" cried Agatha. "The car—"̠

"Hit me," said Grandma, quietly. "Yes. And threw me in the air and tumbled me over and for a few moments there was a severe concussion of circuitries. I might have feared a disconnection, if fear is the word. But then I sat up and gave myself a shake and the few molecules of paint, jarred loose on one printed path or another, magnetized back in position and resilient creature that I am, unbreakable thing that I am, *here* I am."

"I thought you were—" said Agatha.

70   "And only natural," said Grandma. "I mean, anyone else, hit like that, tossed like that. But, O my dear Agatha, not me. And now I see why you were afraid and never trusted me. You didn't know. And I had not as yet proved my singular ability to survive. How dumb of me not to have thought to show you. Just a second." Somewhere in her head, her body, her being, she fitted together some invisible tapes, some old information made new by interblending. She nodded. "Yes. There. A book of child-raising, laughed at by some few people years back when the woman who wrote the book said, as final advice to parents: 'Whatever you do, don't die. Your children will never forgive you.'"

"Forgive," some one of us whispered.

71   "For how can children understand when you just up and go away and never come back again with no excuse, no apologies, no sorry note, nothing."

"They can't," I said.

"So," said Grandma, kneeling down with us beside Agatha who sat up now, new tears brimming her eyes, but a different kind of tears, not tears that drowned, but tears that washed clean. "So your mother ran away to death. And after that, how *could* you trust anyone? If everyone left, vanished finally, who *was* there to trust? So when I came, half wise, half ignorant, I should have known, I did not know, why you would not accept me. For, very simply and honestly, you feared I might not stay, that I lied, that I was vulnerable, too. And two leavetakings, two deaths, were one too many in a single year. But now, do you *see,* Abigail?"

72 "Agatha," said Agatha, without knowing she corrected.

"Do you understand, I shall always, always be here?"

"Oh, yes," cried Agatha, and broke down into a solid weeping in which we all joined, huddled together and cars drew up and stopped to see just how many people were hurt and how many people were getting well right there. End of story.

73 Well, not quite the end.

We lived happily ever after.

Or rather we lived together, Grandma, Agatha-Agamemnon-Abigail, Timothy, and I, Tom, and Father, and Grandma calling us to frolic in great fountains of Latin and Spanish and French, in great seaborne gouts of poetry like Moby Dick sprinkling the deeps with his Versailles jet somehow lost in calms and found in storms; Grandma a constant, a clock, a pendulum, a face to tell all time by at noon, or in the middle of sick nights when, raved with fever, we saw her forever by our beds, never gone, never away, always waiting, always speaking kind words, her cool hand icing our hot brows, the tappet of her uplifted forefinger upsprung to let a twine of cold mountain water touch our flannel tongues. Ten thousand dawns she cut our wildflower lawn, ten thousand nights she wandered, remembering the dust molecules that fell in the still hours before dawn, or sat whispering some lesson she felt needed teaching to our ears while we slept snug.

Until at last, one by one, it was time for us to go away to school, and when at last the youngest, Agatha, was all packed, why Grandma packed, too.

On the last day of summer that last year, we found Grandma down in the front room with various packets and suitcases, knitting, waiting, and though she had often spoken of it, now that the time came we were shocked and surprised.

"Grandma!" we all said. "What are you doing?"

"Why going off to college, in a way, just like you," she said. "Back to Guido Fantoccini's, to the Family."

"The Family?"

74 "Of Pinocchios, that's what he called us for a joke, at first. The Pinocchios and himself Gepetto. And then later gave us his own name: the Fantoccini. Anyway, you have been my family here. Now I go back to my even larger family there, my brothers, sisters, aunts, cousins, all robots who—"

"Who do *what?*" asked Agatha.

75   "It all depends," said Grandma. "Some stay, some linger. Others go to be drawn and quartered, you might say, their parts distributed to other machines who have need of repairs. They'll weigh and find me wanting or not wanting. It may be I'll be just the one they need tomorrow and off I'll go to raise another batch of children and beat another batch of fudge."

76   "Oh, they mustn't draw and quarter you!" cried Agatha.

"No!" I cried, with Timothy.

"My allowance," said Agatha, "I'll pay anything . . . ?"

Grandma stopped rocking and looked at the needles and the pattern of bright yarn. "Well, I wouldn't have said, but now you ask and I'll tell. For a very *small* fee, there's a room, the room of the Family, a large dim parlor, all quiet and nicely decorated, where as many as thirty or forty of the Electric Women sit and rock and talk, each in her turn. I have not been there. I am, after all, freshly born, comparatively new. For a small fee, very small, each month and year, that's where I'll be, with all the others like me, listening to what they've learned of the world and, in my turn, telling how it was with Tom and Tim and Agatha and how fine and happy we were. And I'll tell all I learned from you."

77   "But . . . you taught *us!*"

"Do you *really* think that?" she said. "No, it was turnabout, roundabout, learning both ways. And it's all in here, everything you flew into tears about or laughed over, why, I have it all. And I'll tell it to the others just as they tell their boys and girls and life to me. We'll sit there, growing wiser and calmer and better every year and every year, ten, twenty, thirty years. The Family knowledge will double, quadruple, the wisdom will not be lost. And we'll be waiting there in that sitting room, should you ever need us for your own children in time of illness, or God prevent, deprivation or death. There we'll be, growing old but not old, getting closer to the time, perhaps, someday, when we live up to our first strange joking name."

"The Pinocchios?" asked Tim.

Grandma nodded.

78   I knew what she meant. The day when, as in the old tale, Pinocchio had grown so worthy and so fine that the gift of life had been given him. So I saw them, in future years, the entire family of Fantoccini, the Pinocchios, trading and re-trading, murmuring and whispering their knowledge in the great parlors of philosophy, waiting for the day. The day that could never come.

Grandma must have read that thought in our eyes.

"We'll see," she said. "Let's just wait and see."

79   "Oh, Grandma," cried Agatha and she was weeping as she had wept many years before. "You don't have to wait. You're alive. You've always been alive to us!"

And she caught hold of the old woman and we all caught hold for a long moment and then ran off up in the sky to faraway schools and years and her last words to us before we let the helicopter swarm us away into autumn were these:

"When you are very old and gone childish-small again, with childish ways and childish yens and, in need of feeding, make a wish for the old teacher nurse, the dumb yet wise companion, send for me. I will come back. We shall inhabit the nursery again, never fear."

"Oh, we shall never be old!" we cried. "That will never happen!"

"Never! Never!"

80   And we were gone.

And the years are flown.

And we are old now, Tim and Agatha and I.

Our children are grown and gone, our wives and husbands vanished from the earth and now, by Dickensian coincidence, accept it as you will or not accept, back in the old house, we three.

I lie here in the bedroom which was my childish place seventy, O seventy, believe it, seventy years ago. Beneath this wallpaper is another layer and yet another-times-three to the old wallpaper covered over when I was nine. The wallpaper is peeling. I see peeking from beneath, old elephants, familiar tigers, fine and amiable zebras, irascible crocodiles. I have sent for the paperers to carefully remove all but that last layer. The old animals will live again on the walls, revealed.

And we have sent for someone else.

The three of us have called:

Grandma! You said you'd come back when we had need.

We are surprised by age, by time. We are old. We *need*.

And in three rooms of a summer house very late in time, three old children rise up, crying out in their heads: We *loved* you! We *love* you!

There! There! in the sky, we think, waking at morn. Is that the delivery machine? Does it settle to the lawn?

There! There on the grass by the front porch. Does the mummy case arrive?

Are our names inked on ribbons wrapped about the lovely form beneath the golden mask?!

And the kept gold key, forever hung on Agatha's breast, warmed and waiting? Oh God, will it, after all these years, will it wind, will it set in motion, will it, dearly, *fit*?!

Discussion

1. What clues to Agatha's character do you find in passages 2 and 9? How would you expect her to react to the "electric grandmother"? How does she react?
2. What are Tom's expectations? How are they different from Agatha's?
3. How do the Fantocinni people prepare the children to accept the "electric grandmother" (passages 13 through 22)? How successful are they? Why?
4. What does the "electric grandmother" herself do to win each of the children? How well does she succeed?
5. Why does Agatha refuse to love the "electric grandmother"? What has to happen before she can change her point of view?
6. In passage 70, the "electric grandmother" says, "Whatever you do, don't die. Your children will never forgive you." Do you agree? Why or why not? Do you think the resolution of Agatha's conflict is believable (passages 70 through 72)? Why or why not?
7. Reread passages 50 and 51. What does the "electric grandmother" say about "Those lies . . . that people tell and pretend that they are truths absolute." Can you think of any other "lying truths"?
8. Why does Tom think the day the Pinnochios are waiting for will never come (passage 78)?

9. Agatha says (passage 79), "You don't have to wait. You're alive. You've always been alive to us!" What does it mean to be alive? How can a machine be alive?
10. Below is the first stanza of a poem by Walt Whitman from which the title of this story was taken:

> I sing the body electric,
> The armies of those I love engirth me and I engirth them,
> They will not let me off till I go with them, respond to them,
> And discorrupt them, and charge them full with the charge of the soul.

What do you think "discorrupt" means? How does the poem apply to the Bradbury story? Why?

Writing Assignment 2

You are Fantocinni's chief robotics expert. A complaint has been lodged by an irate customer claiming that your grandmother robots are not realistic enough. "The 'electric grandmother's' ability to change her physical appearance to match the person she is with is not human," the complaint reads. "Real people are always themselves; they are not chameleons, always changing to fit their environment."

If you agree with this complaint, your writing task is to write a description of a new model of the "electric grandmother," explaining how this model reacts "humanly" to the people she meets. Describe the way humans react to one another, and show how this new model is more "human" than the old "electric grandmother."

If you don't agree with the complaint, write a response to the complaining customer in which you explain the "electric grandmother's" reaction to people as essentially human. Think of examples of "real" people changing to meet the people that they meet.

In either case, it may be helpful to you to observe how you and your friends behave with different people, and note what changes do or do not occur. You might also reread passages 33, 35, and 37 of "I Sing the Body Electric" to refresh your memory of the "electric grandmother's" reactions to each of the three children.

The Lottery

by Shirley Jackson

1   The morning of June 27th was clear and sunny, with
the fresh warmth of a full-summer day; the flowers were
blossoming profusely and the grass was richly green. The
people of the village began to gather in the square, between the post office and the bank, around ten o'clock; in
some towns there were so many people that the lottery
took two days and had to be started on June 26th, but in
this village, where there were only about three hundred
people, the whole lottery took only about two hours, so it
could begin at ten o'clock in the morning and still be
through in time to allow the villagers to get home for noon
dinner.

2   The children assembled first, of course. School was
recently over for the summer, and the feeling of liberty
sat uneasily on most of them; they tended to gather together quietly for a while before they broke into bois-
terous play, and their talk was still of the classroom and
the teacher, of books and reprimands. Bobby Martin had
already stuffed his pockets full of stones, and the other
boys soon followed his example, selecting the smoothest
and roundest stones; Bobby and Harry Jones and Dickie
Delacroix—the villagers pronounced this name "Della-
croy"—eventually made a great pile of stones in one
corner of the square and guarded it against the raids of
the other boys. The girls stood aside, talking among themselves, looking over their shoulders at the boys, and the
very small children rolled in the dust or clung to the hands
of their older brothers or sisters.

3   Soon the men began to gather, surveying their own
children, speaking of planting and rain, tractors and taxes.
They stood together, away from the piles of stones in the
corner, and their jokes were quiet and they smiled rather
than laughed. The women, wearing faded house dresses
and sweaters, came shortly after their menfolk. They
greeted one another and exchanged bits of gossip as they
went to join their husbands. Soon the women, standing
by their husbands, began to call to their children, and
the children came reluctantly, having to be called four
or five times. Bobby Martin ducked under his mother's
grasping hand and ran, laughing, back to the pile of
stones. His father spoke up sharply, and Bobby came

quickly and took his place between his father and his oldest brother.

4   The lottery was conducted—as were the square dances, the teen-age club, the Halloween program—by Mr. Summers, who had time and energy to devote to civic activities. He was a round-faced, jovial man and he ran the coal business, and people were sorry for him, because he had no children and his wife was a scold. When he arrived in the square, carrying the black wooden box, there was a murmur of conversation among the villagers, and he waved and called, "Little late today, folks." The postmaster, Mr. Graves, followed him, carrying a three-legged stool, and the stool was put in the center of the square and Mr. Summers set the black box down on it. The villagers kept their distance, leaving a space between themselves and the stool, and when Mr. Summers said, "Some of you fellows want to give me a hand?" there was a hesitation before two men, Mr. Martin and his oldest son, Baxter, came forward to hold the box steady on the stool while Mr. Summers stirred up the papers inside it.

5   The original paraphernalia for the lottery had been lost long ago, and the black box now resting on the stool had been put into use even before Old Man Warner, the oldest man in town, was born. Mr. Summers spoke frequently to the villagers about making a new box, but no one liked to upset even as much tradition as was represented by the black box. There was a story that the present box had been made with some pieces of the box that had preceded it, the one that had been constructed when the first people settled down to make a village here. Every year, after the lottery, Mr. Summers began talking again about a new box, but every year the subject was allowed to fade off without anything's being done. The black box grew shabbier each year; by now it was no longer completely black but splintered badly along one side to show the original wood color, and in some places faded or stained.

6   Mr. Martin and his oldest son, Baxter, held the black box securely on the stool until Mr. Summers had stirred the papers thoroughly with his hand. Because so much of the ritual had been forgotten or discarded, Mr. Summers had been successful in having slips of paper substituted for the chips of wood that had been used for

generations. Chips of wood, Mr. Summers had argued, had been all very well when the village was tiny, but now that the population was more than three hundred and likely to keep on growing, it was necessary to use something that would fit more easily into the black box. The night before the lottery, Mr. Summers and Mr. Graves made up the slips of paper and put them into the box, and it was then taken to the safe of Mr. Summers' coal company and locked up until Mr. Summers was ready to take it to the square next morning. The rest of the year, the box was put away, sometimes one place, sometimes another; it had spent one year in Mr. Graves's barn and another year underfoot in the post office, and sometimes it was set on a shelf in the Martin grocery and left there.

7   There was a great deal of fussing to be done before Mr. Summers declared the lottery open. There were the lists to make up—of heads of families, heads of households in each family, members of each household in each family. There was the proper swearing-in of Mr. Summers by the postmaster, as the official of the lottery; at one time, some people remembered, there had been a recital of some sort, performed by the official of the lottery, a perfunctory, tuneless chant that had been rattled off duly each year; some people believed that the official of the lottery used to stand just so when he said or sang it; others believed that he was supposed to walk among the people; but years and years ago this part of the ritual had been allowed to lapse. There had been, also, a ritual salute, which the official of the lottery had had to use in addressing each person who came up to draw from the box, but this also had changed with time, until now it was felt necessary only for the official to speak to each person approaching. Mr. Summers was very good at all this; in his clean white shirt and blue jeans, with one hand resting carelessly on the black box, he seemed very proper and important as he talked interminably to Mr. Graves and the Martins.

8   Just as Mr. Summers finally left off talking and turned to the assembled villagers, Mrs. Hutchinson came hurriedly along the path to the square, her sweater thrown over her shoulders, and slid into place in the back of the crowd. "Clean forgot what day it was," she said to Mrs. Delacroix, who stood next to her, and they both laughed softly. "Thought my old man was out back stacking

wood," Mrs. Hutchinson went on, "and then I looked out the window and the kids was gone, and then I remembered it was the twenty-seventh and came a-running." She dried her hands on her apron, and Mrs. Delacroix said, "You're in time, though. They're still talking away up there."

9   Mrs. Hutchinson craned her neck to see through the crowd and found her husband and children standing near the front. She tapped Mrs. Delacroix on the arm as a farewell and began to make her way through the crowd. The people separated good-humoredly to let her through; two or three people said, in voices loud enough to be heard across the crowd, "Here comes your Mrs., Hutchinson," and "Bill, she made it after all." Mrs. Hutchinson reached her husband, and Mr. Summers, who had been waiting, said cheerfully, "Thought we were going to have to get on without you, Tessie." Mrs. Hutchinson said, grinning, "Wouldn't have me leave m'dishes in the sink, now, would you, Joe?" and soft laughter ran through the crowd as the people stirred back into position after Mrs. Hutchinson's arrival.

10   "Well, now," Mr. Summers said soberly, "guess we better get started, get this over with, so's we can go back to work. Anybody ain't here?"

"Dunbar," several people said. "Dunbar, Dunbar."

Mr. Summers consulted his list. "Clyde Dunbar," he said. "That's right. He's broke his leg, hasn't he? Who's drawing for him?"

"Me, I guess," a woman said, and Mr. Summers turned to look at her. "Wife draws for her husband," Mr. Summers said. "Don't you have a grown boy to do it for you, Janey?" Although Mr. Summers and everyone else in the village knew the answer perfectly well, it was the business of the official of the lottery to ask such questions formally. Mr. Summers waited with an expression of polite interest while Mrs. Dunbar answered.

"Horace's not but sixteen yet," Mrs. Dunbar said regretfully. "Guess I gotta fill in for the old man this year."

"Right," Mr. Summers said. He made a note on the list he was holding. Then he asked, "Watson boy drawing this year?"

11   A tall boy in the crowd raised his hand. "Here," he said. "I'm drawing for m'mother and me." He blinked his eyes nervously and ducked his head as several voices in the crowd said things like "Good fellow, Jack," and "Glad to see your mother's got a man to do it."

"Well," Mr. Summers said, "guess that's everyone. Old Man Warner make it?"

"Here," a voice said, and Mr. Summers nodded.

12 A sudden hush fell on the crowd as Mr. Summers cleared his throat and looked at the list. "All ready?" he called. "Now, I'll read the names—heads of families first —and the men come up and take a paper out of the box. Keep the paper folded in your hand without looking at it until everyone has had a turn. Everything clear?"

13 The people had done it so many times that they only half listened to the directions; most of them were quiet, wetting their lips, not looking around. Then Mr. Summers raised one hand high and said, "Adams." A man disengaged himself from the crowd and came forward. "Hi, Steve," Mr. Summers said, and Mr. Adams said, "Hi, Joe." They grinned at one another humorlessly and nervously. Then Mr. Adams reached into the black box and took out a folded paper. He held it firmly by one corner as he turned and went hastily back to his place in the crowd, where he stood a little apart from his family, not looking down at his hand.

14 "Allen," Mr. Summers said. "Anderson. . . . Bentham."

"Seems like there's no time at all between lotteries any more," Mrs. Delacroix said to Mrs. Graves in the back row. "Seems like we got through with the last one only last week."

"Time sure goes fast," Mrs. Graves said.

"Clark. . . . Delacroix."

"There goes my old man," Mrs. Delacroix said. She held her breath while her husband went forward.

"Dunbar," Mr. Summers said, and Mrs. Dunbar went steadily to the box while one of the women said, "Go on, Janey," and another said, "There she goes."

"We're next," Mrs. Graves said. She watched while Mr. Graves came around from the side of the box, greeted Mr. Summers gravely, and selected a slip of paper from the box. By now, all through the crowd there were men holding the small folded papers in their large hands, turning them over and over nervously. Mrs. Dunbar and her two sons stood together, Mrs. Dunbar holding the slip of paper.

"Harburt. . . . Hutchinson."

"Get up there, Bill," Mrs. Hutchinson said, and the people near her laughed.

"Jones."

15   "They do say," Mr. Adams said to Old Man Warner, who stood next to him, "that over in the north village they're talking of giving up the lottery."

    Old Man Warner snorted. "Pack of crazy fools," he said. "Listening to the young folks, nothing's good enough for them. Next thing you know, they'll be wanting to go back to living in caves, nobody work any more, live *that* way for a while. Used to be a saying about 'Lottery in June, corn be heavy soon.' First thing you know, we'd all be eating stewed chickweed and acorns. There's always been a lottery," he added petulantly. "Bad enough to see young Joe Summers up there joking with everybody."

    "Some places have already quit lotteries," Mrs. Adams said.

    "Nothing but trouble in that," Old Man Warner said stoutly. "Pack of young fools."

16   "Martin." And Bobby Martin watched his father go forward. "Overdyke.... Percy."

    "I wish they'd hurry," Mrs. Dunbar said to her older son. "I wish they'd hurry."

    "They're almost through," her son said.

    "You get ready to run tell Dad," Mrs. Dunbar said.

    Mr. Summers called his own name and then stepped forward precisely and selected a slip from the box. Then he called, "Warner."

    "Seventy-seventh year I been in the lottery," Old Man Warner said as he went through the crowd. "Seventy-seventh time."

    "Watson." The tall boy came awkwardly through the crowd. Someone said, "Don't be nervous, Jack," and Mr. Summers said, "Take your time, son."

    "Zanini."

17   After that, there was a long pause, a breathless pause, until Mr. Summers, holding his slip of paper in the air, said, "All right, fellows." For a minute, no one moved, and then all the slips of paper were opened. Suddenly, all the women began to speak at once, saying, "Who is it?" "Who's got it?" "Is it the Dunbars?" "Is it the Watsons?" Then the voices began to say, "It's Hutchinson. It's Bill," "Bill Hutchinson's got it."

    "Go tell your father," Mrs. Dunbar said to her older son.

    People began to look around to see the Hutchinsons.

Bill Hutchinson was standing quiet, staring down at the paper in his hand. Suddenly, Tessie Hutchinson shouted to Mr. Summers, "You didn't give him time enough to take any paper he wanted. I saw you. It wasn't fair!"

"Be a good sport, Tessie," Mrs. Delacroix called, and Mrs. Graves said, "All of us took the same chance."

"Shut up, Tessie," Bill Hutchinson said.

18   "Well, everyone," Mr. Summers said, "that was done pretty fast, and now we've got to be hurrying a little more to get done in time." He consulted his next list. "Bill," he said, "you draw for the Hutchinson family. You got any other households in the Hutchinsons?"

"There's Don and Eva." Mrs. Hutchinson yelled. "Make *them* take their chance."

"Daughters draw with their husbands' families, Tessie," Mr. Summers said gently. "You know that as well as anyone else."

"It wasn't *fair*," Tessie said.

"I guess not, Joe," Bill Hutchinson said regretfully. "My daughter draws with her husband's family, that's only fair. And I've got no other family except the kids."

"Then, as far as drawing for families is concerned, it's. you," Mr. Summers said in explanation, "and as far as drawing for households is concerned, that's you, too. Right?"

"Right," Bill Hutchinson said.

"How many kids, Bill?" Mr. Summers asked formally.

"Three," Bill Hutchinson said. "There's Bill, Jr., and Nancy, and little Dave. And Tessie and me."

"All right, then," Mr. Summers said. "Harry, you got their tickets back?"

Mr. Graves nodded and held up the slips of paper. "Put them in the box, then," Mr. Summers directed. "Take Bill's and put it in."

"I think we ought to start over," Mrs. Hutchinson said, as quietly as she could. "I tell you it wasn't *fair*. You didn't give him time enough to choose. *Everybody* saw that."

19   Mr. Graves had selected the five slips and put them in the box, and he dropped all the papers but those onto the ground, where the breeze caught them and lifted them off.

"Listen, everybody," Mrs. Hutchinson was saying to the people around her.

"Ready, Bill?" Mr. Summers asked, and Bill Hutchinson, with one quick glance around at his wife and children, nodded.

"Remember," Mr. Summers said, "take the slips and keep them folded until each person has taken one. Harry, you help little Dave." Mr. Graves took the hand of the little boy, who came willingly with him up to the box. "Take a paper out of the box, Davy," Mr. Summers said. Davy put his hand into the box and laughed. "Take just one paper," Mr. Summers said. "Harry, you hold it for him." Mr. Graves took the child's hand and removed the folded paper from the tight fist and held it while little Dave stood next to him and looked up at him wonderingly.

"Nancy next," Mr. Summers said. Nancy was twelve, and her school friends breathed heavily as she went forward, switching her skirt, and took a slip daintily from the box. "Bill, Jr.," Mr. Summers said, and Billy, his face red and his feet overlarge, nearly knocked the box over as he got a paper out. "Tessie," Mr. Summers said. She hesitated for a minute, looking around defiantly, and then set her lips and went up to the box. She snatched a paper out and held it behind her.

"Bill," Mr. Summers said, and Bill Hutchinson reached into the box and felt around, bringing his hand out at last with the slip of paper in it.

20   The crowd was quiet. A girl whispered, "I hope it's not Nancy," and the sound of the whisper reached the edges of the crowd.

"It's not the way it used to be," Old Man Warner said clearly. "People ain't the way they used to be."

"All right," Mr. Summers said. "Open the papers. Harry, you open little Dave's."

21   Mr. Graves opened the slip of paper and there was a general sigh through the crowd as he held it up and everyone could see that it was blank. Nancy and Bill, Jr., opened theirs at the same time, and both beamed and laughed, turning around to the crowd and holding their slips of paper above their heads.

"Tessie," Mr. Summers said. There was a pause, and then Mr. Summers looked at Bill Hutchinson, and Bill unfolded his paper and showed it. It was blank.

"It's Tessie," Mr. Summers said, and his voice was hushed. "Show us her paper, Bill."

22   Bill Hutchinson went over to his wife and forced the

slip of paper out of her hand. It had a black spot on it, the black spot Mr. Summers had made the night before with the heavy pencil in the coal-company office. Bill Hutchinson held it up, and there was a stir in the crowd.

"All right, folks," Mr. Summers said. "Let's finish quickly."

23   Although the villagers had forgotten the ritual and lost the original black box, they still remembered to use stones. The pile of stones the boys had made earlier was ready; there were stones on the ground with the blowing scraps of paper that had come out of the box. Mrs. Delacroix selected a stone so large she had to pick it up with both hands and turned to Mrs. Dunbar. "Come on," she said. "Hurry up."

Mrs. Dunbar had small stones in both hands, and she said, gasping for breath, "I can't run at all. You'll have to go ahead and I'll catch up with you."

The children had stones already, and someone gave little Davy Hutchinson a few pebbles.

24   Tessie Hutchinson was in the center of a cleared space by now, and she held her hands out desperately as the villagers moved in on her. "It isn't fair," she said. A stone hit her on the side of the head.

Old Man Warner was saying, "Come on, come on, everyone." Steve Adams was in the front of the crowd of villagers, with Mrs. Graves beside him.

25   "It isn't fair, it isn't right," Mrs. Hutchinson screamed, and then they were upon her.

Writing Assignment 3

As soon as you finish reading "The Lottery" (and without discussing the story with any of your classmates), write a short paper in which you describe your reaction to the events in the story as if you had arrived in the village just as they were taking place. Describe as vividly as you can the thoughts that go through your mind. Is there anything in your previous experience to help you understand the events? As a stranger, how do you act? What do you think of the people? of the situation?

After writing your paper, exchange it with some of your classmates. Then, in small groups, you might want to discuss their reactions to your reactions: did everyone react differently? similarly? Why? How effective do they think you were in conveying your reactions?

In addition, several students in succession may want to read their papers to the class, as if they were all in the crowd at the same time and giving you an opportunity to listen in to their thoughts.

Discussion

1. Is the time of the story the far past, the recent past, or the present? Give reasons for your answer.
2. Reread passages 1 through 4. How would you characterize the mood of this story? What kind of mood do the people seem to be in? Give specific examples.
3. In passage 5 (and in later parts of the story) there is a reference to tradition. How would you define tradition in general? What is the specific tradition in this story? How does a sense of tradition affect the people in the story? Are people in real life similarly affected by tradition? Give several specific examples.
4. How would you describe Mrs. Hutchinson's attitude toward the lottery in passages 8 through 9? From what she says and the way she acts at this point in the story, how would you describe her previous experiences with the lottery? How have they shaped her attitude?
5. What do Mr. Summers' comments in the first paragraph of passage 10 indicate about his attitude toward the lottery? In passages 10 through 14, what other attitudes are expressed by various people that tell us something about their points of view? How are these attitudes similar to, or different from, Mrs. Hutchinson's? Do these attitudes make the result of the lottery seem more or less horrible than a deliberate, malicious killing would be?
6. Discuss the conversation between Old Man Warner and Mr. and Mrs. Adams in passage 15. Do their comments remind you of anything outside the story in real life? If so, what?
7. In passages 17 and 18, how does Mrs. Hutchinson's attitude change? Is her response realistic? How would you

respond? How do you think the other people in the story would respond? Explain your answers.

8. What clues to character are given by the way each member of the family acts (passage 19) as he draws his slip? To what extent do you think age and experience explain the actions and reactions of Nancy and Bill? of Mr. Hutchinson? Can you think of any other reasons to explain their behavior? How "realistic" is it?

9. Discuss both parts of Mrs. Hutchinson's last statement, "It isn't fair, it isn't right." Do you agree with her on both points? Why or why not? How does his statement indicate a change in her point of view?

10. Using the story as a reference point, discuss the various ways in which people are affected by community experience (tradition) and by personal experience. How are the effects different? How are they similar?

Writing Assignment 4 (*optional*)

After you have discussed the papers from Writing Assignment 2 and the preceding questions, go back to the story again. Look into the mind of one of the characters in the story and describe what you believe he might have been thinking while the lottery was in progress. Have several students use the same character. Then, in a small group discussion, compare and contrast the results in order to discover how different students described the thoughts of the same character and why they felt that character would be having the thoughts they put into his or her head. Such a comparison would suggest what factors in the story and in each student-author's point of view had a significant effect on what he wrote. A class reading of several papers might shed further light on the subject.

Writing Assignment 5

Your task in this assignment is once again to look back upon your past experiences to find one that stands out, for one reason or another, as significant. This time, however, recount the event not from the perspective of the time when it actually happened, but from your point of view now. How and why has your point of view changed because of the experiences that have come between the event you are describing and the point in time from which you are now describing it? (Think, for instance, how Nancy and Bill Hutchinson might see the events of the lottery five or ten years after they actually took place, or how Jim might view his first day of school as an adult.)

We have all had experiences that change in their significance after the passage of time. How many times has something happened to us that doesn't seem important until long after? Or conversely, how many times has an incident (breaking up with a boy friend or girl friend, losing a big game, having an argument or a fight with our best friend) seemed disastrous at the time, but not so important later on?

What you need to do for this assignment is recall such an incident and write about it from your present point of view, discovering for yourself and conveying to your reader what it means to you now, how that meaning is different from what it was then, and why and how your experiences have affected your point of view.

Chapter 5

The View
from up There

"Man is a social animal."—*Seneca*

"It is impossible, in our condition of Society, not to be sometimes a Snob."—*William Makepeace Thackeray*

"To get into the best society nowadays, one has either to feed people, amuse people, or shock people."—*Oscar Wilde*

"There are four varieties in society; the lovers, the ambitious, observers, and fools. The fools are the happiest."—*Hippolyte A. Taine*

"Society is no comfort to one not sociable."—*William Shakespeare*

"Let us move forward together into the Great Society." —*Lyndon Baines Johnson*

"Society Is Sick."—*title of a magazine article*

THE WORLD YOU LIVE IN

Like many words in the English language, *society* is easier to talk about than to define. From the beginning of recorded history, people have praised and accepted, criticized and rejected, cussed and discussed society. But what is it? Perhaps this definition from *Funk & Wagnalls Standard College Dictionary* will help.

so·ci′e·ty (sə·sī′ə·tē) *n. pl.* ·ties 1. The system of community life in which individuals form a continuous and regulatory association for their mutual benefit and protection. 2. The body of persons composing such a community; also, all people collectively, regarded as having certain common characteristics and relationships. 3. A number of persons in a community regarded as forming a class having certain common interests, similar status, etc. 4. The fashionable or aristocratic portion of a community, considered as a class; also, their activities, manner of life, etc. 5. A body of persons associated for a common purpose or object; an association: a medical *society*. 6. *U.S.* In some States, an incorporated religious congregation. 7. A club or fraternity. 8. Association based on friendship or intimacy; companionship; also, one's friends or associates. 9. *Ecol.* A group of plants or animals living together under the same physiographic conditions and influences. *Abbr. soc.* [< OF *societe* < L *societas, -tatis* < *socius* friend]

As you read about the society that Jem and Scout Finch try to understand in Chapter 11 from *To Kill a Mockingbird*, which dictionary definition of society would you apply to the town of Maycomb?

from To Kill a Mockingbird
by Harper Lee

1   When we were small, Jem and I confined our activities to the southern neighborhood, but when I was well into the second grade at school and tormenting Boo Radley became passé, the business section of Maycomb drew us frequently up the street past the real property of Mrs. Henry Lafayette Dubose. It was impossible to go to town without passing her house unless we wished to walk a mile out of the way. Previous minor encounters with her left me with no desire for more, but Jem said I had to grow up some time.

Mrs. Dubose lived alone except for a Negro girl in constant attendance, two doors up the street from us in a house with steep front steps and a dog-trot hall. She was very old; she spent most of each day in bed and the rest of it in a wheelchair. It was rumored that she kept a CSA pistol concealed among her numerous shawls and wraps.

2   Jem and I hated her. If she was on the porch when we passed, we would be raked by her wrathful gaze, subjected to ruthless interrogation regarding our behavior, and given a melancholy prediction on what we would

amount to when we grew up, which was always nothing. We had long ago given up the idea of walking past her house on the opposite side of the street; that only made her raise her voice and let the whole neighborhood in on it.

We could do nothing to please her. If I said as sunnily as I could, "Hey, Mrs. Dubose," I would receive for an answer, "Don't you say hey to me, you ugly girl! You say good afternoon, Mrs. Dubose!"

3   She was vicious. Once she heard Jem refer to our father as "Atticus" and her reaction was apoplectic. Besides being the sassiest, most disrespectful mutts who ever passed her way, we were told that it was quite a pity our father had not remarried after our mother's death. A lovelier lady than our mother never lived, she said, and it was heartbreaking the way Atticus Finch let her children run wild. I did not remember our mother, but Jem did—he would tell me about her sometimes—and he went livid when Mrs. Dubose shot us this message.

Jem, having survived Boo Radley, a mad dog and other terrors, had concluded that it was cowardly to stop at Miss Rachel's front steps and wait, and had decreed that we must run as far as the post office corner each evening to meet Atticus coming from work. Countless evenings Atticus would find Jem furious at something Mrs. Dubose had said when we went by.

4   "Easy does it, son," Atticus would say. "She's an old lady and she's ill. You just hold your head high and be a gentleman. Whatever she says to you, it's your job not to let her make you mad."

Jem would say she must not be very sick, she hollered so. When the three of us came to her house, Atticus would sweep off his hat, wave gallantly to her and say, "Good evening, Mrs. Dubose! You look like a picture this evening."

I never heard Atticus say like a picture of what. He would tell her the courthouse news, and would say he hoped with all his heart she'd have a good day tomorrow. He would return his hat to his head, swing me to his shoulders in her very presence, and we would go home in the twilight. It was times like these when I thought my father, who hated guns and had never been to any wars, was the bravest man who ever lived.

5   The day after Jem's twelfth birthday his money was burning up his pockets, so we headed for town in the

early afternoon. Jem thought he had enough to buy a miniature steam engine for himself and a twirling baton for me.

I had long had my eye on that baton: it was at V. J. Elmore's, it was bedecked with sequins and tinsel, it cost seventeen cents. It was then my burning ambition to grow up and twirl with the Maycomb County High School band. Having developed my talent to where I could throw up a stick and almost catch it coming down, I had caused Calpurnia to deny me entrance to the house every time she saw me with a stick in my hand. I felt that I could overcome this defect with a real baton, and I thought it generous of Jem to buy one for me.

6   Mrs. Dubose was stationed on her porch when we went by.

"Where are you two going at this time of day?" she shouted. "Playing hooky, I suppose. I'll just call up the principal and tell him!" She put her hands on the wheels of her chair and executed a perfect right face.

"Aw, it's Saturday, Mrs. Dubose," said Jem.

"Makes no difference if it's Saturday," she said obscurely. "I wonder if your father knows where you are?"

"Mrs. Dubose, we've been goin' to town by ourselves since we were this high." Jem placed his hand palm down about two feet above the sidewalk.

"Don't you lie to me!" she yelled. "Jeremy Finch, Maudie Atkinson told me you broke down her scuppernong arbor this morning. She's going to tell your father and then you'll wish you never saw the light of day! If you aren't sent to the reform school before next week, my name's not Dubose!"

Jem, who hadn't been near Miss Maudie's scuppernong arbor since last summer, and who knew Miss Maudie wouldn't tell Atticus if he had, issued a general denial.

"Don't you contradict me!" Mrs. Dubose bawled. "And *you*—" she pointed an arthritic finger at me—"what are you doing in those overalls? You should be in a dress and camisole, young lady! You'll grow up waiting on tables if somebody doesn't change your ways—a Finch waiting on tables at the O.K. Café—hah!"

7   I was terrified. The O.K. Café was a dim organization on the north side of the square. I grabbed Jem's hand but he shook me loose.

"Come on, Scout," he whispered. "Don't pay any at-

tention to her, just hold your head high and be a gentleman."

But Mrs. Dubose held us: "Not only a Finch waiting
on tables but one in the courthouse lawing for niggers!"

Jem stiffened. Mrs. Dubose's shot had gone home and
she knew it:

"Yes indeed, what has this world come to when a
Finch goes against his raising? I'll tell you!" She put her
hand to her mouth. When she drew it away, it trailed a
long silver thread of saliva. "Your father's no better than
the niggers and trash he works for!"

8   Jem was scarlet. I pulled at his sleeve, and we were
followed up the sidewalk by a philippic on our family's
moral degeneration, the major premise of which was that
half the Finches were in the asylum anyway, but if our
mother were living we would not have come to such a
state.

I wasn't sure what Jem resented most, but I took
umbrage at Mrs. Dubose's assessment of the family's
mental hygiene. I had become almost accustomed to hearing insults aimed at Atticus. But this was the first one
coming from an adult. Except for her remarks about Atticus, Mrs. Dubose's attack was only routine. There was
a hint of summer in the air—in the shadows it was cool,
but the sun was warm, which meant good times coming:
no school and Dill.

9   Jem bought his steam engine and we went by Elmore's for my baton. Jem took no pleasure in his acquisi-
tion; he jammed it in his pocket and walked silently
beside me toward home. On the way home I nearly hit
Mr. Link Deas, who said, "Look out now, Scout!" when
I missed a toss, and when we approached Mrs. Dubose's
house my baton was grimy from having picked it up out
of the dirt so many times.

She was not on the porch.

10   In later years, I sometimes wondered exactly what
made Jem do it, what made him break the bonds of "You
just be a gentleman, son," and the phase of self-conscious
rectitude he had recently entered. Jem had probably
stood as much guff about Atticus lawing for niggers as
had I, and I took it for granted that he kept his temper—
he had a naturally tranquil disposition and a slow fuse.
At the time, however, I thought the only explanation for
what he did was that for a few minutes he simply went
mad.

What Jem did was something I'd do as a matter of course had I not been under Atticus's interdict, which I assumed included not fighting horrible old ladies. We had just come to her gate when Jem snatched my baton and ran flailing wildly up the steps into Mrs. Dubose's front yard, forgetting everything Atticus had said, forgetting that she packed a pistol under her shawls, forgetting that if Mrs. Dubose missed, her girl Jessie probably wouldn't.

He did not begin to calm down until he had cut the tops off every camellia bush Mrs. Dubose owned, until the ground was littered with green buds and leaves. He bent my baton against his knee, snapped it in two and threw it down.

By that time I was shrieking. Jem yanked my hair, said he didn't care, he'd do it again if he got a chance, and if I didn't shut up he'd pull every hair out of my head. I didn't shut up and he kicked me. I lost my balance and fell on my face. Jem picked me up roughly but looked like he was sorry. There was nothing to say.

11   We did not choose to meet Atticus coming home that evening. We skulked around the kitchen until Calpurnia threw us out. By some voo-doo system Calpurina seemed to know all about it. She was a less than satisfactory source of palliation, but she did give Jem a hot biscuit-and-butter which he tore in half and shared with me. It tasted like cotton.

We went to the living room. I picked up a football magazine, found a picture of Dixie Howell, showed it to Jem and said, "This looks like you." That was the nicest thing I could think to say to him, but it was no help. He sat by the windows, hunched down in a rocking chair, scowling, waiting. Daylight faded.

12   Two geological ages later, we heard the soles of Atticus's shoes scrape the front steps. The screen door slammed, there was a pause—Atticus was at the hat rack in the hall—and we heard him call, "Jem!" His voice was like the winter wind.

Atticus switched on the ceiling light in the living room and found us there, frozen still. He carried my baton in one hand; its filthy yellow tassel trailed on the rug. He held out his other hand; it contained fat camellia buds.

"Jem," he said, "are you responsible for this?"

"Yes sir."

"Why'd you do it?"

Jem said softly, "She said you lawed for niggers and trash."

"You did this because she said that?"

Jem's lips moved, but his, "Yes sir," was inaudible.

"Son, I have no doubt that you've been annoyed by your contemporaries about me lawing for niggers, as you say, but to do something like this to a sick old lady is inexcusable. I strongly advise you to go down and have a talk with Mrs. Dubose," said Atticus. "Come straight home afterward."

Jem did not move.

"Go on, I said."

I followed Jem out of the living room. "Come back here," Atticus said to me. I came back.

13 Atticus picked up the *Mobile Press* and sat down in the rocking chair Jem had vacated. For the life of me, I did not understand how he could sit there in cold blood and read a newspaper when his only son stood an excellent chance of being murdered with a Confederate Army relic. Of course Jem antagonized me sometimes until I could kill him, but when it came down to it he was all I had. Atticus did not seem to realize this, or if he did he didn't care.

I hated him for that, but when you are in trouble you become easily tired: soon I was hiding in his lap and his arms were around me.

"You're mighty big to be rocked," he said.

"You don't care what happens to him," I said. "You just send him on to get shot at when all he was doin' was standin' up for you."

14 Atticus pushed my head under his chin. "It's not time to worry yet," he said. "I never thought Jem'd be the one to lose his head over this—thought I'd have more trouble with you."

I said I didn't see why we had to keep our heads anyway, that nobody I knew at school had to keep his head about anything.

"Scout," said Atticus, "when summer comes you'll have to keep your head about far worse things . . . it's not fair for you and Jem, I know that, but sometimes we have to make the best of things, and the way we conduct ourselves when the chips are down—well, all I can say is, when you and Jem are grown, maybe you'll look back on this with some compassion and some feeling that I didn't let you down. This case, Tom Robinson's case, is something that goes to the essence of a man's conscience—Scout, I couldn't go to church and worship God if I didn't try to help that man."

15　"Atticus, you must be wrong. . . ."

"How's that?"

"Well, most folks seem to think they're right and you're wrong. . . ."

"They're certainly entitled to think that, and they're entitled to full respect for their opinions," said Atticus, "but before I can live with other folks I've got to live with myself. The one thing that doesn't abide by majority rule is a person's conscience."

16　When Jem returned, he found me still in Atticus's lap. "Well, son?" said Atticus. He set me on my feet, and I made a secret reconnaissance of Jem. He seemed to be all in one piece, but he had a queer look on his face. Perhaps she had given him a dose of calomel.

"I cleaned it up for her and said I was sorry, but I ain't, and that I'd work on 'em every Saturday and try to make 'em grow back out."

"There was no point in saying you were sorry if you aren't," said Atticus. "Jem, she's old and ill. You can't hold her responsible for what she says and does. Of course, I'd rather she'd have said it to me than to either of you, but we can't always have our 'druthers." [1]

17　Jem seemed fascinated by a rose in the carpet. "Atticus," he said, "she wants me to read to her."

"Read to her?"

"Yes sir. She wants me to come every afternoon after school and Saturdays and read to her out loud for two hours. Atticus, do I have to?"

"Certainly."

"But she wants me to do it for a month."

"Then you'll do it for a month."

Jem planted his big toe delicately in the center of the rose and pressed it in. Finally he said, "Atticus, it's all right on the sidewalk but inside it's—it's all dark and creepy. There's shadows and things on the ceiling. . . ."

Atticus smiled grimly. "That should appeal to your imagination. Just pretend you're inside the Radley house."

18　The following Monday afternoon Jem and I climbed the steep front steps to Mrs. Dubose's house and padded

[1] *have our 'druthers:* have our choice.

down the open hallway. Jem, armed with *Ivanhoe* and full of superior knowledge, knocked at the second door on the left.

"Mrs. Dubose?" he called.

Jessie opened the wood door and unlatched the screen door.

"Is that you, Jem Finch?" she said. "You got your sister with you. I don't know—"

"Let 'em both in, Jessie," said Mrs. Dubose. Jessie admitted us and went off to the kitchen.

19   An oppressive odor met us when we crossed the threshold, an odor I had met many times in rain-rotted gray houses where there are coal-oil lamps, water dippers, and unbleached domestic sheets. It always made me afraid, expectant, watchful.

In the corner of the room was a brass bed, and in the bed was Mrs. Dubose. I wondered if Jem's activities had put her there, and for a moment I felt sorry for her. She was lying under a pile of quilts and looked almost friendly.

There was a marble-topped washstand by her bed; on it were a glass with a teaspoon in it, a red ear syringe, a box of absorbent cotton, and a steel alarm clock standing on three tiny legs.

20   "So you brought that dirty little sister of yours, did you?" was her greeting.

Jem said quietly, "My sister ain't dirty and I ain't scared of you," although I noticed his knees shaking.

I was expecting a tirade, but all she said was, "You may commence reading, Jeremy."

Jem sat down in a cane-bottom chair and opened *Ivanhoe*. I pulled up another one and sat beside him.

"Come closer," said Mrs. Dubose. "Come to the side of the bed."

We moved our chairs forward. This was the nearest I had ever been to her, and the thing I wanted most to do was move my chair back again.

21   She was horrible. Her face was the color of a dirty pillowcase, and the corners of her mouth glistened with wet, which inched like a glacier down the deep grooves enclosing her chin. Old-age liver spots dotted her cheeks, and her pale eyes had black pinpoint pupils. Her hands were knobby, and the cuticles were grown up over her fingernails. Her bottom plate was not in, and her upper lip protruded; from time to time she would draw her

nether lip to her upper plate and carry her chin with it. This made the wet move faster.

I didn't look any more than I had to. Jem reopened *Ivanhoe* and began reading. I tried to keep up with him, but he read too fast. When Jem came to a word he didn't know, he skipped it, but Mrs. Dubose would catch him and make him spell it out. Jem read for perhaps twenty minutes, during which time I looked at the soot-stained mantelpiece, out the window, anywhere to keep from looking at her. As he read along, I noticed that Mrs. Dubose's corrections grew fewer and farther between, that Jem had even left one sentence dangling in mid-air. She was not listening.

I looked toward the bed.

Something had happened to her. She lay on her back, with the quilts up to her chin. Only her head and shoulders were visible. Her head moved slowly from side to side. From time to time she would open her mouth wide, and I could see her tongue undulate faintly. Cords of saliva would collect on her lips; she would draw them in, then open her mouth again. Her mouth seemed to have a private existence of its own. It worked separate and apart from the rest of her, out and in, like a clam hole at low tide. Occasionally it would say, "Pt," like some viscous substance coming to a boil.

22   I pulled Jem's sleeve.

He looked at me, then at the bed. Her head made its regular sweep toward us, and Jem said, "Mrs. Dubose, are you all right?" She did not hear him.

The alarm clock went off and scared us stiff. A minute later, nerves still tingling, Jem and I were on the sidewalk headed for home. We did not run away, Jessie sent us: before the clock wound down she was in the room pushing Jem and me out of it.

"Shoo," she said, "you all go home."

Jem hesitated at the door.

"It's time for her medicine," Jessie said. As the door swung shut behind us I saw Jessie walking quickly toward Mrs. Dubose's bed.

23   It was only three forty-five when we got home, so Jem and I drop-kicked in the back yard until it was time to meet Atticus. Atticus had two yellow pencils for me and a football magazine for Jem, which I suppose was a silent reward for our first day's session with Mrs. Dubose. Jem told him what happened.

"Did she frighten you?" asked Atticus.

"No sir," said Jem, "but she's so nasty. She has fits or somethin'. She spits a lot."

"She can't help that. When people are sick they don't look nice sometimes."

"She scared me," I said.

Atticus looked at me over his glasses. "You don't have to go with Jem, you know."

24 The next afternoon at Mrs. Dubose's was the same as the first, and so was the next, until gradually a pattern emerged: everything would begin normally—that is, Mrs. Dubose would hound Jem for a while on her favorite subjects, her camellias and our father's nigger-loving propensities; she would grow increasingly silent, then go away from us. The alarm clock would ring, Jessie would shoo us out, and the rest of the day was ours.

25 "Atticus," I said one evening, "what exactly is a nigger-lover?"

Atticus's face was grave. "Has somebody been calling you that?"

"No sir, Mrs. Dubose calls you that. She warms up every afternoon calling you that. Francis called me that last Christmas, that's where I first heard it."

"Is that the reason you jumped on him?" asked Atticus.

"Yes sir . . ."

"Then why are you asking me what it means?"

I tried to explain to Atticus that it wasn't so much what Francis said that had infuriated me as the way he had said it. "It was like he'd said snot-nose or somethin'."

"Scout," said Atticus, "nigger-lover is just one of those terms that don't mean anything—like snot-nose. It's hard to explain—ignorant, trashy people use it when they think somebody's favoring Negroes over and above themselves. It's slipped into usage with some people like ourselves, when they want a common, ugly term to label somebody."

26 "You aren't really a nigger-lover, then, are you?"

"I certainly am. I do my best to love everybody . . . I'm hard put, sometimes—baby, it's never an insult to be called what somebody thinks is a bad name. It just shows you how poor that person is, it doesn't hurt you. So don't let Mrs. Dubose get you down. She has enough troubles of her own."

27 One afternoon a month later Jem was ploughing his

way through Sir Walter Scout, as Jem called him, and Mrs. Dubose was correcting him at every turn, when there was a knock on the door. "Come in!" she screamed.

Atticus came in. He went to the bed and took Mrs. Dubose's hand. "I was coming from the office and didn't see the children," he said. "I thought they might still be here."

Mrs. Dubose smiled at him. For the life of me I could not figure out how she could bring herself to speak to him when she seemed to hate him so. "Do you know what time it is, Atticus?" she said. "Exactly fourteen minutes past five. The alarm clock's set for five-thirty. I want you to know that."

It suddenly came to me that each day we had been staying a little longer at Mrs. Dubose's, that the alarm clock went off a few minutes later every day, and that she was well into one of her fits by the time it sounded. Today she had antagonized Jem for nearly two hours with no intention of having a fit, and I felt hopelessly trapped. The alarm clock was the signal for our release; if one day it did not ring, what would we do?

28 "I have a feeling that Jem's reading days are numbered," said Atticus.

"Only a week longer, I think," she said, "just to make sure ..."

Jem rose. "But—"

Atticus put out his hand and Jem was silent. On the way home, Jem said he had to do it just for a month and the month was up and it wasn't fair.

"Just one more week, son," said Atticus.

"No," said Jem.

"Yes," said Atticus.

29 The following week found us back at Mrs. Dubose's. The alarm clock had ceased sounding, but Mrs. Dubose would release us with, "That'll do," so late in the afternoon Atticus would be home reading the paper when we returned. Although her fits had passed off, she was in every other way her old self: when Sir Walter Scott became involved in lengthy descriptions of moats and castles, Mrs. Dubose would become bored and pick on us:

"Jeremy Finch, I told you you'd live to regret tearing up my camellias. You regret it now, don't you?"

Jem would say he certainly did.

"Thought you could kill my Snow-on-the-Mountain,

did you? Well, Jessie says the top's growing back out. Next time you'll know how to do it right, won't you? You'll pull it up by the roots, won't you?"

Jem would say he certainly would.

"Don't you mutter at me, boy! You hold up your head and say yes ma'am. Don't guess you feel like holding it up, though, with your father what he is."

Jem's chin would come up, and he would gaze at Mrs. Dubose with a face devoid of resentment. Through the weeks he had cultivated an expression of polite and detached interest, which he would present to her in answer to her most blood-curdling inventions.

At last the day came. When Mrs. Dubose said, "That'll do," one afternoon, she added, "and that's all. Good-day to you."

30   It was over. We bounded down the sidewalk on a spree of sheer relief, leaping and howling.

That spring was a good one: the days grew longer and gave us more playing time. Jem's mind was occupied mostly with the vital statistics of every college football player in the nation. Every night Atticus would read us the sports pages of the newspapers. Alabama might go to the Rose Bowl again this year, judging from its prospects, not one of whose names we could pronounce. Atticus was in the middle of Windy Seaton's column one evening when the telephone rang.

He answered it, then went to the hat rack in the hall. "I'm going down to Mrs. Dubose's for a while," he said. "I won't be long."

31   But Atticus stayed away until long past my bedtime. When he returned he was carrying a candy box. Atticus sat down in the living room and put the box on the floor beside his chair.

"What'd she want?" asked Jem.

We had not seen Mrs. Dubose for over a month. She was never on the porch any more when we passed.

"She's dead, son," said Atticus. "She died a few minutes ago."

"Oh," said Jem. "Well."

"Well is right," said Atticus. "She's not suffering any more. She was sick for a long time. Son, didn't you know what her fits were?"

Jem shook his head.

32   "Mrs. Dubose was a morphine addict," said Atticus.

"She took it as a pain-killer for years. The doctor put her on it. She'd have spent the rest of her life on it and died without so much agony, but she was too contrary—"

"Sir?" said Jem.

Atticus said, "Just before your escapade she called me to make her will. Dr. Reynolds told her she had only a few months left. Her business affairs were in perfect order but she said, 'There's still one thing out of order.'"

"What was that?" Jem was perplexed.

"She said she was going to leave this world beholden to nothing and nobody. Jem, when you're sick as she was, it's all right to take anything to make it easier, but it wasn't all right for her. She said she meant to break herself of it before she died, and that's what she did."

Jem said, "You mean that's what her fits were?"

"Yes, that's what they were. Most of the time you were reading to her I doubt if she heard a word you said. Her whole mind and body were concentrated on that alarm clock. If you hadn't fallen into her hands, I'd have made you go read to her anyway. It may have been some distraction. There was another reason—"

"Did she die free?" asked Jem.

"As the mountain air," said Atticus. "She was conscious to the last, almost. Conscious," he smiled, "and cantankerous. She still disapproved heartily of my doings, and said I'd probably spend the rest of my life bailing you out of jail. She had Jessie fix you this box—"

33   Atticus reached down and picked up the candy box. He handed it to Jem.

Jem opened the box. Inside, surrounded by wads of damp cotton, was a white, waxy, perfect camellia. It was a Snow-on-the-Mountain.

Jem's eyes nearly popped out of his head. "Old hell-devil, old hell-devil!" he screamed, flinging it down. "Why can't she leave me alone?"

In a flash Atticus was up and standing over him. Jem buried his face in Atticus's shirt front. "Sh-h," he said. "I think that was her way of telling you—everything's all right now, Jem, everything's all right. You know, she was a great lady."

34   "A lady?" Jem raised his head. His face was scarlet. "After all those things she said about you, a lady?"

"She was. She had her own views about things, a lot different from mine, maybe . . . son, I told you that if you hadn't lost your head I'd have made you go read to her.

I wanted you to see something about her—I wanted you to see what real courage is, instead of getting the idea that courage is a man with a gun in his hand. It's when you know you're licked before you begin but you begin anyway and you see it through no matter what. You rarely win, but sometimes you do. Mrs. Dubose won, all ninety-eight pounds of her. According to her views, she died beholden to nothing and nobody. She was the bravest person I ever knew."

Jem picked up the candy box and threw it in the fire. He picked up the camellia, and when I went off to bed I saw him fingering the wide petals. Atticus was reading the paper.

Discussion

1. From whose point of view is this story told? How does the narrator react to Mrs. Dubose? Why? How old do you think the narrator is? Give reasons for your answer. How do you feel about Mrs. Dubose after reading passages 1 through 3?

2. The narrator refers to her father as Atticus. What does this tell you about the relationship between them? What does Mrs. Dubose think about children who refer to their father by his first name? How does Atticus treat Mrs. Dubose? What effect does his treatment of her have on the narrator?

3. How does Mrs. Dubose feel about black people? About white people who work for black people? How does Jem react to Mrs. Dubose? Why? How do you feel about Mrs. Dubose after reading passages 6 and 7? What specific words or phrases do you react most strongly to? Why?

4. How does Jem "break the bonds of 'You just be a gentleman, son,' and the phase of self-conscious rectitude he had recently entered"? What does this sentence mean?

5. What kind of man is Atticus Finch? How does he feel about what he is doing for Tom Robinson? Is he concerned about the community's attitude toward his children because he is defending Tom Robinson? Explain your answer. According to Atticus, what does the term "nigger-lover" mean, who uses it, and why do they use it?

6. How do you feel about Mrs. Dubose after reading passage 21? Do you have your own impression of Mrs. Dubose in her sickbed, or do you see her only as Scout sees her? Why?

7. How does Jem's reaction to Mrs. Dubose's "most blood-curdling inventions" change before she dies? Why does he call her an "old hell-devil" when he opens the candy box? Why did Mrs. Dubose put the Snow-on-the-Mountain inside the box?
8. How do you feel about Mrs. Dubose after reading passages 32 through 34? Why do you think you learn about her courage from Atticus instead of from Scout? What do you think Jem is thinking and feeling when he fingers the white petals of the camellia? Give reasons for your answers.
9. Which of the dictionary definitions of "society" would you say best describes Mrs. Dubose's idea of the word? Which best describes Atticus's? Explain your answer.

SOME COMMENTS ON SOCIETY

The question that preceded Chapter 11 from *To Kill a Mockingbird* may have troubled you. "As you read about the society that Jem and Scout Finch try to understand, which dictionary definition of society would you apply to the town of Maycomb?"

As you read the chapter, you might have asked, "What do one old lady, a couple of kids, and their father have to do with society? How can I apply a dictionary definition of society to the chapter?"

Taken in its narrowest sense, a neighborhood can be a society. The people in the neighborhood are "the body of persons composing a . . . community"—definition 2 from the dictionary entry on page 89.

If we analyze that definition further, we find that society is "a number of persons in a community regarded as forming a class having certain common interests, similar status, etc." Consider the relationship of Mrs. Dubose with the Finches: They live in the same neighborhood; Mrs. Dubose lives "two doors up the street" from the Finches. Mrs. Dubose had obviously at one time been a woman of considerable influence in the community, and Atticus is certainly an influential—though controversial—lawyer. Mrs. Dubose tries to impose her views of how people should behave in society on Scout and Jem, and she comments on why she thinks Atticus is breaking her social code: "Not only a Finch [referring to Scout] waiting on tables but one in the courthouse lawing for niggers!"

Although they have many "common interests" and "similar status," the values of Mrs. Dubose and Atticus are not necessarily similar. The attitudes of Mrs. Dubose reflect a segment of society which permits a "lady" to speak of "lawing for niggers" (with all that this phrase implies) while she is attended by a black woman in her own home. Atticus, on the other hand, obviously feels that as a responsible member of society he must be sensitive to the needs and aspirations of all people, black and white. By defending a black man, he tries, in his own way, to bring justice for all to Maycomb.

Scout and Jem are children growing up in a society they do not always understand, because a society—"a body of persons in a community"—is not always easy to comprehend, composed as it is of people ranging from a Mrs. Dubose to an Atticus Finch with all kinds of people in between and on both sides.

Thus, this chapter from *To Kill a Mockingbird* gives one view of one slice of society in the town of Maycomb.

Writing Assignment 1

You have probably had the experience of using a word in conversation and having your listener ask you to define it. There are many words in the English language to which you give distinct meanings because of your experiences with the people, actions, or things that the words represent. For example, what meanings would you give to the italicized words in these sentences?

Jeremy is a *conservative*.

Eleanor is a *liberal*.

Pauline is a *moderate*.

Senator X is a *radical*.

You can look up the definition of each of those italicized words in a dictionary, and you can probably find one that comes close to what you mean when you use the word to describe someone's politics. But can you give your definition of *liberal* or *conservative*, for example, in six or eight words as lexicographers, or compilers of dictionaries, do? Probably not. When lexicographers define words, they try to give the meanings that most people attach to words, and they try to define them in as few words as possible. The limitations of space do not permit them to give complete definitions of words like *liberal, conservative, moderate,* and *radical.* Entire chapters of books, and even entire books, have been devoted to definitions of *liberal* and *conservative.* Even then, those who consider themselves liberals or conservatives may read these books and feel that the definitions are not accurate or inclusive.

Like *liberal* and *conservative, society* is a word that you probably do not define in exactly the same way a friend might. What is *society?* Do you live in a society, or do you live in several societies, according to the definition of the word on pages 89–90?

Your writing task here is to define the word *society* so that your reader will know exactly what *you* mean if you were to write: "If I am to take my place in *society*, I must . . ."

Before you attempt to define the word, ask yourself questions like the following:

1. What do other people mean by *society* when they say:
   Society demands that I do (this or that).
   I want to take my rightful place in *society*.
   Society frowns on the criminal.
   Society does not accept the non-conformist.
   What would I mean by *society* if I used the same sentences?
2. How does my definition differ from other people's? Why?
3. What can I tell my reader about *society*, as I define it, to help him understand what I mean?

Your writing task, then, is to define *society* so thoroughly that your reader will understand exactly what you mean when you use the word.

Writing Assignment 2

Does the society in which you live help shape your point of view? To what extent do you share the values of your society? Do you sometimes deliberately say or do things to make certain you will be an accepted member of your society?

What sorts of things? In short: to what extent has your society shaped you; to what extent are you what you are because of the influence of society?

Your writing task here is to explain as completely as you can to the same reader (the one for whom you wrote the definition of *society*) how society has influenced the formation and development of your point of view.

Writing Assignment 3

You have probably heard people refer to society as if it were a small, elite group of people who run the city, the state, or even the country. When you hear the term used that way, you may envision people who are rich, snobbish perhaps, and powerful. Sometimes these people may be referred to as *high society*. They are the so-called uppercrust who, according to some people, view the rest of the world from a kind of high hill, or even a mountain.

Is there a *high society* in your city or community? What do you mean by that term? To whom does it apply? Do the members of *high society* have any influence over you?

In a letter to a friend, explain what *high society* is in your community and how it influences you.

Writing Assignment 4

During the early 1970's some critics of American society wrote that it was "sick." Do you believe that present-day society is sick or healthy or some combination of the two? What are your reasons?

You have been asked to give a speech before a group of adults. Explain why you think that society is sick or healthy, and tell your audience what you think people must do to make society well (if you think it is sick) or what they must do to keep society well (if you think it is not sick).

Chapter 6

The He
and
The She
of It

LITTLE GIRLS
DON'T CLIMB TREES

"Stop that, Amelia," Mother screamed. "You know that little girls play with dolls—not with cars and trucks."

"You can't be a policeman, Bernice. That's a man's job, and you live in a man's world."

"Your daughter is such a sweet little girl. She'll be a darling wife for some man."

"Women don't go to college to learn—but to get a husband."

Some of those quotations may sound all too familiar if you are a girl. Perhaps you have heard comments like those from well-meaning friends and relatives who think that girls have primarily one duty in society—to become wives and mothers.

Consider the following comments from a boy's point of view:

"Stop crying, Gerald. Little men never cry."

"Work hard, Homer. If you save enough money, you'll find yourself a pretty young wife."

"You can't major in home economics, Archie. That's for girls."

"Get a haircut, Richard. You're beginning to look like a girl."

Writing Assignment 1

Describe an incident in which you became very unhappy because of limitations imposed upon you in the name of "femininity" or "masculinity." Following are a few questions that may help you decide on an incident you can describe:

1. Have I ever been told that I could not play a certain game because of my sex? Who told me? Why did he or she tell me that? How did it make me feel? What did I do? If I played the game anyway, what was the reaction of the person who told me not to play?
2. Have I ever been involved in conversations in which I was told what I could or could not do when I grow up because of my sex? Who told me? Why? What did he or she say? What did I say? Why? Did I say anything, or did I just accept the other person's advice? If I accepted it without comment, why did I?

In describing the incident, make certain that your reader, a person your own age, can picture the people talking and can understand why they speak as they do. Let your reader know how you felt at the time without simply telling him that you were unhappy. Describe your actions and/or tell your reader what you were thinking.

What It Would Be Like If Women Win
by Gloria Steinem

1   Any change is fearful, especially one affecting both politics and sex roles, so let me begin these utopian [1] speculations with a fact. To break the ice.

Women don't want to exchange places with men. Male chauvinists, [2] science-fiction writers and comedians may favor that idea for its shock value, but psychologists say it is a fantasy based on ruling-class ego and guilt. Men assume that women want to imitate them, which is just what white people assumed about blacks. An assumption so strong that it may convince the second-class group of the need to imitate, but for both women and blacks that stage has passed. Guilt produces the question: What

[1] *utopian:* ideal; perfect.
[2] *chauvinist:* a person having an unfairly discriminating attachment to a group to which he belongs—in this case, the male sex.

if they could treat us as we have treated them?

2   That is not our goal. But we do want to change the economic system to one more based on merit. In Women's Lib Utopia, there will be free access to good jobs—and decent pay for the bad ones women have been performing all along, including housework. Increased skilled labor might lead to a four-hour workday, and higher wages would encourage further mechanization of repetitive jobs now kept alive by cheap labor.

3   With women as half the country's elected representatives, and a woman President once in a while, the country's *machismo* [3] problems would be greatly reduced. The old-fashioned idea that manhood depends on violence and victory is, after all, an important part of our troubles in the streets, and in Viet Nam. I'm not saying that women leaders would eliminate violence. We are not more moral than men; we are only uncorrupted by power so far. When we do acquire power, we might turn out to have an equal impulse toward aggression. Even now, Margaret Mead believes that women fight less often but more fiercely than men, because women are not taught the rules of the war game and fight only when cornered. But for the next fifty years or so, women in politics will be very valuable for tempering the idea of manhood into something less aggressive and better suited to this crowded, post-atomic planet. Consumer protection and children's rights, for instance, might get more legislative attention.

     Men will have to give up ruling-class privileges, but in return they will no longer be the only ones to support the family, get drafted, bear the strain of power and responsibility. Freud to the contrary, anatomy is not destiny, at least not for more than nine months at a time. In Israel, women are drafted, and some have gone to war. In England, more men type and run switchboards. In India and Israel, a woman rules. In Sweden, both parents take care of the children. In this country, come Utopia, men and women won't reverse roles; they will be free to choose according to individual talents and preferences. . . .

4   In order to produce that kind of confidence and individuality, child rearing will train according to talent. Little girls will no longer be surrounded by air-tight, self-fulfilling prophecies of natural passivity, lack of ambition and objectivity, inability to exercise power, and dexterity (so long as special aptitude for jobs requiring patience

[3] *machismo:* masculine pride.

and dexterity is confined to poorly paid jobs; brain surgery is for males).

5   Schools and universities will help to break down traditional sex roles, even when parents will not. Half the teachers will be men, a rarity now at preschool and elementary levels; girls will not necessarily serve cookies or boys hoist up the flag. Athletic teams will be picked only by strength and skill. Sexually segregated courses like auto mechanics and home economics will be taken by boys and girls together. New courses in sexual politics will explore female subjugation as the model for political oppression, and women's history will be an academic staple, along with black history, at least until the white-male-oriented textbooks are integrated and rewritten.

6   As for the American child's classic problem—too much mother, too little father—that would be cured by an equalization of parental responsibility. Free nurseries, school lunches, family cafeterias built into every housing complex, service companies that will do household cleaning chores in a regular, businesslike way, and more responsibility by the entire community for the children: all these will make it possible for both mother and father to work, and to have equal leisure time with the children at home. For parents of very young children, however, a special job category, created by Government and unions, would allow such parents a shorter workday.

The revolution would not take away the option of being a housewife. A woman who prefers to be her husband's housekeeper and/or hostess would receive a percentage of his pay determined by the domestic relations courts. If divorced, she might be eligible for a pension fund, and for a job-training allowance. Or a divorce could be treated the same way that the dissolution of a business partnership is now.

7   If these proposals seem farfetched, consider Sweden, where most of them are already in effect. Sweden is not yet a working Women's Lib model; most of the role-reform programs began less than a decade ago, and are just beginning to take hold. But that country is so far ahead of us in recognizing the problem that Swedish statements on sex and equality sound like bulletins from the moon.

Our marriage laws, for instance, are so reactionary that Women's Lib groups want couples to take a compulsory written exam on the law, as for a driver's license, before going through with the wedding. A man has alimony and wifely debts to worry about, but a woman may lose so many of her civil rights that in the U.S. now, in important legal ways, she becomes a child again. In some states, she cannot sign credit agreements, use her maiden name, incorporate a business, or establish a legal residence of her own. Being a wife, according to most social and legal definitions, is still a 19th century thing.

8   Assuming, however, that these blatantly sexist laws are abolished or reformed, that job discrimination is forbidden, that parents share financial responsibility for each other and the children, and that sexual relationships become partnerships of equal adults (some pretty big assumptions), then marriage will probably go right on. Men and women are, after all, physically complementary. When society stops encouraging men to be exploiters and women to be parasites, they may turn out to be more complementary in emotion as well. Women's Lib is not trying to destroy the American family. A look at the statistics on divorce—plus the way in which old people are farmed out with strangers and young people flee the home—shows the destruction that has already been done. Liberated women are just trying to point out the disaster, and build compassionate and practical alternatives from the ruins.

What will exist is a variety of alternative life-styles. Since the population explosion dictates that childbearing be kept to a minimum, parents-and-children will be only one of many "families": couples, age groups, working groups, mixed communes, blood-related clans, class groups, creative groups. Single women will have the right to stay single without ridicule, without the attitudes now betrayed by "spinster" and "bachelor."

9   Changes that now seem small may get bigger:

MEN'S LIB. Men now suffer from more diseases due to stress, heart attacks, ulcers, a higher suicide rate, greater difficulty living alone, less adaptability to change and, in general, a shorter life span than women. There is some scientific evidence that what produces physical problems is not work itself, but the inability to choose which work, and how much. With women bearing half the financial responsibility, and with the idea of "masculine" jobs gone, men might well feel freer and live longer.

10   RELIGION. Protestant women are already becoming

ordained ministers; radical nuns are carrying out liturgical functions that were once the exclusive property of priests; Jewish women are rewriting prayers—particularly those that Orthodox Jews recite every morning thanking God they are not female. In the future, the church will become an area of equal participation by women. This means, of course, that organized religion will have to give up one of its great historical weapons: sexual repression. In most structured faiths, from Hinduism through Roman Catholicism, the status of women went down as the position of priests ascended. Male clergy implied, if they did not teach, that women were unclean, unworthy, and sources of ungodly temptation, in order to remove them as rivals for the emotional forces of men. Full participation of women in ecclesiastical life might involve certain changes in theology, such as, for instance, a radical redefinition of sin.

11   LITERARY PROBLEMS. Revised sex roles will outdate more children's books than civil rights ever did. Only a few children had the problem of a *Little Black Sambo,* but most have the male-female stereotypes of "Dick and Jane." A boomlet of children's books about mothers who work has already begun, and liberated parents and editors are beginning to pressure for change in the textbook industry. Fiction writing will change more gradually, but romantic novels with wilting heroines and swashbuckling heroes will be reduced to historical value. (*Marjorie Morningstar,* a romantic novel that took the '50s by storm, has already begun to seem as unreal as its '20s predecessor, *The Sheik.*) As for the literary plots that turn on forced marriages or horrific abortions, they will seem as dated as Prohibition stories. . . .

12   MANNERS AND FASHION. Dress will be more androgynous,[1] with class symbols becoming more important than sexual ones. Pro- or anti-Establishment styles may already be more vital than who is wearing them. Hardhats are just as likely to rough up antiwar girls as antiwar men in the street, and police understand that women are just as likely to be pushers as bombers. Dances haven't required that one partner lead the other for years, anyway. Chivalry will transfer itself to those who need it, or deserve respect: old people, admired people, anyone with an armload of packages. Women with normal work identities will be less likely to attach their whole sense of self

[4] *androgynous:* both male and female.

to youth and appearance; thus there will be fewer nervous breakdowns when the first wrinkles appear. Lighting cigarettes and other treasured niceties will become gestures of mutual affection. "I like to be helped on with my coat," says one Women's Lib worker, "but not if it costs me $2,000 a year in salary."

13   For those with nostalgia for a simpler past, here is a word of comfort. Anthropologist Geoffrey Gorer studied the few peaceful human tribes and discovered one common characteristic: sex roles were not polarized. Differences of dress and occupation were at a minimum. Society, in other words, was not using sexual blackmail as a way of getting women to do cheap labor, or men to be aggressive.

Thus Women's Lib may achieve a more peaceful society on the way toward its other goals. That is why the Swedish government considers reform to bring about greater equality in the sex roles one of its most important concerns. As Prime Minister Olof Palme explained in a widely ignored speech delivered in Washington this spring: "It is *human beings* we shall emancipate. In Sweden today, if a politician should declare that the woman ought to have a different role from man's, he would be regarded as something from the Stone Age." In other words, the most radical goal of the movement is egalitarianism.

If Women's Lib wins, perhaps we all do.

Discussion

1. According to Miss Steinem, what is the goal of the Women's Lib movement? What is the popular misconception of the goal? What are some of the reasons for the misconception?

2. Reread the first paragraph in passage 3. Why do you agree or disagree with the opinions expressed by Miss Steinem in that paragraph?

3. What is the meaning of "anatomy is not destiny"? What evidence does Miss Steinem offer to prove this statement? If you believe that "anatomy is destiny," explain why.

4. What do you think Miss Steinem means by "child rearing will train according to talent"? What evidence does she offer to suggest that little girls are not now trained ac-

cording to talent? What additional evidence can you offer? If you disagree, what evidence can you offer to suggest that little girls are being trained according to talent?

5. What do you think this sentence means: "New courses in sexual politics will explore female subjugation as the model for political oppression, and women's history will be an academic staple, along with black history, at least until the white-male-oriented textbooks are integrated and re-written."

   Do you agree or disagree that history textbooks are "white-male-oriented"? What history textbooks can you offer as evidence to support your belief? Why did you choose them?

6. According to passage 6, what will be the future role of the housewife? Of the husband? What evidence does Miss Steinem offer to show that her proposals are practical and effective?

7. Why do you think Miss Steinem writes in passage 7 that "a woman may lose so many of her civil rights that in the U.S. now, in important legal ways, she becomes a child again"?

8. Why, according to Miss Steinem, might men "feel freer and live longer" if the Women's Lib movement wins?

9. How does Miss Steinem think the Women's Lib movement will affect religion? Why will it cause literary problems? How will it affect fashions and manners?

10. What does the author mean by "the most radical goal of the movement is egalitarianism"?

Writing Assignment 2

In passage 8, Miss Steinem writes: "Women's Lib is not trying to destroy the American family." Reread the article and read other articles on the Women's Lib movement. Do you believe the family unit will be strengthened if the movement wins, or do you think the family unit will be weakened or destroyed? What are the reasons for your opinions?

Your writing task here is to write a letter to the editor of a daily newspaper in which you explain why you think the Women's Lib movement will or will not destroy the American family. Your readers are the members of the community in which you live, and your task is to persuade them to accept your point of view. To be convincing, you need to offer as much evidence as you can to support your assertion that the Women's Lib movement will or will not destroy the family unit.

Writing Assignment 3

Write a short story or play in which the action takes place after "women have won." Think of some situation in which you can describe what you think the world will be like then and how you view the victory.

Before you begin to write, you might ask yourself questions like the following:

1. Who is my central character? Can I best picture the world after the Women's Lib movement wins through the eyes of a man or a woman? Should the character reveal the conditions of the time through his thoughts, or should conditions be revealed through description, dialogue, and/ or action? What settings and situations would most effectively portray the differences between women's position now and when my story takes place?
2. If women win, will we still use the titles, *Miss*, *Mrs.*, and *Mr.*? *Mother* and *Father*? Will words and phrases that have traditionally reflected a male-dominated world—*mankind*, *showmanship*—be replaced? What other changes in language might occur? Will we still use masculine pronouns in sentences like "Every student must turn in *his* paper on time"?
3. What roles will men and women play in the home? Who will care for the children? Who will do most of the cooking and cleaning? Who will support the family?
4. Will there be more women in government? Will there be a woman president? Will there be an end to wars?
5. Will the schools change if women win? What changes would have to be made? Why? What courses will be offered? Who will take them?
6. Will women play professional football, basketball, baseball, and hockey—if such sports exist?
7. What, in brief, will the world be like? What do I think of

such a world? How do I see myself fitting into that world?

After you have asked yourself these and other questions, begin thinking about a situation in which you can involve your characters to show clearly the state of the world after women have won. What is happening? How is the world different? How can I express my point of view about it through one of the characters?

Chapter 7

Color My Point
of View "___."

Does your attitude toward another person depend to
some extent on the color of his or her skin? Does the fact
that you are black or brown or red or white or yellow affect
the way you see yourself, other people, and your world? Does
the color of your skin affect the way other people treat you?

The answers to those questions may seem obvious to
you if you have been involved in situations that caused you
to think about them. Otherwise, you might not necessarily
have spent much time wondering how the color of your skin
affects your point of view. Does it make any difference in the
way you think, talk, and act? Think about that question as
you read the following chapter from Conrad Richter's novel,
The Light in the Forest. All you need to know about True
Son is that he is a white boy who was captured and reared
by Delaware Indians and now thinks of himself as one of
them. Del Hardy is a white soldier who was also captured
by the Indians but was returned to his white family.

from The Light in the Forest
by Conrad Richter

1   When Del Hardy saw Fort Pitt through the trees, he
threw his cap in the air. For weeks he had lived among
savages in the wilderness. Now, thank God, he was laying
eyes on a white man's settlement again. Sight of chim-
neys, of the certain slant of roofs with the British flag
flying over them, stirred him deeply inside. These walls of
mortared stone bespoke his own people. English or
French, they had built to stay. This might be their

farthest outpost now, but it wouldn't be long. He had heard a dozen soldiers say they were coming back to clear and settle the rich black land they had found along Yellow Creek beyond the Ohio.

His feet felt light as deer hooves climbing the mountains and jogging down the eastern slopes. He reckoned one of the pleasantest feelings a white man could have was, after tramping days in the everlasting forest, to come out on cleared land and look across open fields. Same way with a road. He had marched nigh onto three hundred miles on savage trails and traces, stumbling over roots and logs, slopping through runs and bogs. Now the hard firm ground of a cartway under foot lifted him up. His eye ran warmly over the good ruts, and the familiar zigzag of rail fences. Tame cattle in the fields stood quiet and decent as they passed. Here neither man nor beast had to be afraid of his shadow. The log barns and sheds on the land had an air of white man's industry and their houses of peace. From all of them young folk and old came to the road to rejoice as the army and its delivered captives passed.

2   That had been a day or two ago. Yesterday at Carlisle the freed white captives had been given back to the bosom of their families. You'd reckon by this time they'd learned to appreciate it. Yet, look at this Butler boy on ahead riding with his father, sullen as a young spider, making as though he didn't understand a word his father said. To watch him and listen to his Indian talk, you'd reckon English a bastard tongue and Delaware the only language fit to put in your mouth. You could see he still reckoned himself a savage and all those were blackguards and slavers who had anything to do with fetching him back to his own people. But then Indians were a strange lot. Del himself had lived neighbors to them as a boy. He knew their ways but never could he make them out.

Thank the Lord, he told himself, when they came to the home river. It would take his mind off the boy for a spell. The great stream flowed south from the mountains, a noble tide a mile wide. Just to let his eye roam over it gave him peace and wonder. The ferry pushing off from the far shore was a mark of civilization and the white race. To the north a squadron of islands swam like ships pointing down stream, and still farther northward were the majestic gaps of the Blue Mountains, one after the other, where the great river poured through.

3　　　It was to Del the greatest sight in his world. The narrower if deeper Ohio couldn't compare to it. And yet when he looked at the boy, he found him sitting in his saddle unnoticing and unmoved. Not till they were on the ferry did he wake up to it. That was when his father called the river Susquehanna. Quickly, as if he had heard that name before, the boy lifted his head. His eyes took in the great stretch of water with the fields and houses on its far shore. Then he poured out bitter words in Delaware.

"What's he saying?" his father asked.

Del made a face.

4　　　"He says the Susquehanna and all the water flowing into it belongs to his Indian people. He says his Indian father lived on its banks to the north. The graves of his ancestors are beside it. He says he often heard his father tell how the river and graves were stolen from them by the white people."

Mr. Butler looked weary.

"Tell him we'll talk about that some other time. Tell him he's getting close to home now. If he'll look up at those hills across the river, he'll see Paxton township where he was born."

5　　　Even before he translated it, Del was sure the boy had understood. He gazed at the far bank with a sudden look of terror.

"Place of Peshtank white men?" he asked in thick, Indian English.

His father looked pleased. He put an affectionate hand on the boy's shoulder.

"That's right, son. Peshtank or Paxton. It's the same thing. We call them the Paxton boys. Many of them, I'm proud to say, are your own kin."

6　　　The boy looked as if a whiplash had hit him. He stared wildly up at the facing hills. The ferryman pushed by with his pole. The water curled around the flat bow of the scow. On the eastern bank, the sycamores and maples grew steadily nearer. Suddenly, before the boat touched shore, the boy kicked his moccasin heels into the sides of his horse and plunged with him into the shallow water. At once he was urging the gray with sharp Indian yells up the high steep bank. By the time Del and Mr. Butler reached the shore level, all they got was a glimpse of horse and boy vanishing into the northern forest.

"They'll stop him at Fort Hunter," the boy's father said.

7   But before reaching the fort, they came on the boy's horse standing riderless in the trail. Del jumped from the saddle and bent over the ground. In the thawed earth he could make out where the gray had shied at a white rag tied to a bush at a fork in the trail. In the ground were marks where the boy had landed. His tracks on foot were harder to follow, but Del ran down a path that led to the river. In a tangle of alders and sweetbrier he stopped and soon pulled out the kicking and biting boy. Mr. Butler had to help drag him back to his horse and lift him on the saddle. Then, with the gray firmly tethered between the two men, they rode back down the river trail.

They passed a mill, open fields, log and stone buildings. Their road climbed the rising hills. Now they could see rich, cleared farms with solid-looking houses and barns. The boy's father turned into a lane lined with young walnuts. Ahead of them a barn with stone ends had the greatest space between them that Del Hardy thought he had ever seen in a building. Nearby was a limestone tenant house and, beyond the spring, a stone mansion house with a wide front door. As the riders approached, a boy and servant girl came out on the porch with a determined-looking woman beside them.

8   Del glanced at Mr. Butler. His face was uneasy. Likely he had looked forward to a time when his son would come back to him. But hardly had he counted on a homecoming like this. It would be an ordeal they would all have to go through.

The two men swung to the ground in front of the house, but the boy had to be ordered from the saddle. Del took him by the arm and led him to the porch steps.

"Your brother is home," the father said uncomfortably to the small boy standing there, then to True Son, "You never saw Gordie. He was born while you were away. But you ought to recollect your Aunt Kate."

9   The older boy stood silent in his Indian dress, ignoring all. The servant girl had started toward him. Now she stopped painfully, while Aunt Kate stared in frank disapproval and disbelief. Only the small boy seemed to see nothing unusual in the scene, gazing at his brother with open delight and admiration.

"Well, let's go in," the father said, clearing his throat, and they moved into the wide hall.

"Harry!" a lady's voice called eagerly from upstairs.

Mr. Butler and Aunt Kate exchanged glances.

"Harry!" the voice called again. "Aren't you bringing him up?"

The father gave a look as if there was no help for it.

"You better come along," he told the soldier significantly, then with the small boy running ahead and the aunt coming after, they urged True Son toward the stairs.

10   It wasn't easy to get him up. Plenty of times, Del knew, this boy must have shinned up cliffs and trees higher than this. But he eyed the stairs and bannister rail as an invention of the devil. For a while the guard figured this short distance from floor to floor might be the hardest part of their journey. Then Gordie, running ahead, turned the tide. He bounced up those steps so easy, looking around as he ran, that his brother shook off the hands that tried to help him. For a moment his eyes measured this white man's ladder, wide enough for two or three men abreast, the oaken treads shaven smooth as an axe handle and polished with a kind of beeswax. Then half crouching and taking two steps at a time, he climbed to the second-floor hall. It ran from one end of the house to the other, with doors branching off on both sides.

"This way, son," Mr. Butler said, and took him toward an open doorway where his smaller brother stood waiting.

11   The room they entered was large and sunny, with green-figured white walls. The broad flooring held much furniture, a red cherry bureau and washstand, a high polished chest of drawers, two or three small tables and twice as many chairs, a large bed with impressive posts, and by the window a couch on which a lady in a blue dressing-gown half sat and half lay. You could tell by the black hair and eyes and by the eager loving look she gave the boy that she was his mother. Just the same his father had to push him to the couch, and for all the notice he took of her, she might not have been there. Only when she pulled down his head and kissed him did he acknowledge her presence, stiffening painfully.

12   "Why, you look like an Indian, John!" she exclaimed. "You even walk like one. You've had a hard

fate, but thank God your life was spared and you're home with us again. Are you happy?"

True Son had wrapped himself again in aloofness like a blanket. His mother turned with quick compassion.

"Doesn't he remember any English?"

"He understands a good deal, we think," his father said. "But not everything. We don't know how much he can talk it. So far he's only said a few words in English. Del has to talk to him in Indian."

"I'm sure he understands me," his mother declared. "I can tell by his eyes when I speak. You do understand me, don't you, John?"

The boy gave no response. She went on quickly, sympathetically.

13   "You've been away a long time, John. Your education has been arrested. You've had to live in heathen darkness and ignorance. Now you must make up for lost time. You're almost a young man. The first and most important thing to know is your native English tongue. We'll start right now. I am your mother, Myra Butler. This is your father, Harry Butler. Your brother is Gordon Butler. And you are John C. Butler. Now repeat it after me. John Cameron Butler."

The boy said nothing, only stood there impassively. Aunt Kate turned from the room as if she could stand no more.

14   "He don't know his own name. He don't even know when it's Sunday," Del heard her tell the servant girl on the stairs.

But back in her bedroom Mrs. Butler had far from given up. She might be an invalid, but you could tell she was the mistress of this house.

"I want you to repeat your name after me. Say John, John!" She seized his arm and shook it, then turned helplessly.

"Maybe he's deaf and dumb, Mamma!" little Gordie said.

That broke the strain for a moment and all smiled, all except the boy in Indian dress. Gradually his insistent, somber silence overtook the others. You could see Mrs. Butler come to a decision.

15   "Very well, John," she said, tightening her lips. "I see you are willful and stubborn as your Uncle Wilse. We will have to act accordingly. Your family and friends

are coming to see you tomorrow and I won't have you standing up crude and ignorant as a savage in front of them. You'll have to stay in this room till you speak your own name."

You could see that the boy understood. Resentment crept into his dark face. He spoke rapidly in Delaware. Del had to translate it.

"He says his name is Lenni Quis. In English you'd call it Original Son or True Son."

Mrs. Butler heard him.

16   "But he's not with the Delawares any more. He's at home under our roof, and here he'll have to recognize his real name."

The boy regarded her with burning dark eyes so like her own.

"True Son my real name," he said in thick English, having trouble with the letter r. "My father and mother give me this name."

"He means his Indian father and mother," Del explained.

Mrs. Butler had flushed.

"Well, I think that will be enough today," she said. "He has spoken a few words in English at any rate."

17   She took from beside her on the couch some clothing she had been mending. A feeling of constriction crept over the boy when he saw they were a pair of light gray Yengwe pantaloons and a youth's yellow jacket. She went on. "When I heard you were coming home, I borrowed these from your cousin Alec. Now I'd like you to put them on and see how they fit you."

The boy made no effort to take them.

"Do you understand, John?" she repeated earnestly. "You're to put these on so we can see what you look like in civilized dress."

The boy stared with loathing at the pants and jacket. They were symbols of all the lies, thefts, and murders by the white man. Now he was asked to wear them. You might as well ask a deer to dress itself in the hide of its enemy, the wolf.

"Do you hear your mother?" Del said sharply and repeated the request in Delaware.

18   The boy still held back. How could he touch these things? Had there been small wood by the fireplace, he might have picked up the clothes with the end of a stick

and carried them out, holding them as far from his body as possible. But there was no stick. Then Gordie took them for him.

"When you put these on, will you give me your Indian clothes, True Son?" he asked eagerly as they went from the room. "Then I can be an Indian."

The older boy did not say anything nor did he take off his Indian dress when they reached the room where Gordie took him, but for a moment a look of mutual respect and understanding passed between the two brothers.

Discussion

1. In the chapter preceding the one reprinted in this book, the reader sees white man's civilization from True Son's point of view.

Never along the Tuscarawas had he seen such tremendous mounds of earth and rock heaped to the sky and running farther than the eye could see. Once behind him, they were like unscalable stockades separating him from his people. And now he saw he had reached a point he had often heard about, the sad, incredible region where the Indian forest had been cut down by the white destroyers and no place left for the Indian game to live. Here the desolate face of the earth had been exposed to dead brown weeds and stubble, lorded over by the lodges of the white people and the fat storehouses of their riches. Fort Pitt had been ugly, but it had still been Indian country. This, now, he knew, was the barbarous homeland of his white enemies.

He could feel them all around him. His moccasins tramped no longer soft mossy forest trails but a hard-rutted roadway. Curious wooden barriers ran alongside in a regular crooked fashion with spreading wooden horns at each angle. He was told they were meant to keep the white man's cattle from running free. The cattle stood tame and stolid as the soldiers passed, but the white people came running from their lodges to line the road. From the noise they made you might have thought the white army came from a great battle with loot and scalps instead of only children captives and without a shot having been fired.

Every hour the forest receded and the lodges of the whites grew more numerous. Late that afternoon they encamped near a white man's village. How could human beings, he wondered, live in such confinement! Here the whites had shut themselves up in prisons of gray stone and of red stone called brick, while the larger log houses had been covered over with smooth painted boards to give them the glittering ostentation and falseness so dear to the whites. Evidently their coming had been expected, for many people awaited them. Herds of saddled horses stood around. Men and women must have come a long way. Small crowds tried to storm the captives as soon as they arrived, but the soldiers held them off.

True Son disliked the sight of white man's civilization; Del Hardy "threw his cap in the air" when he saw Fort Pitt. True Son saw the "desolate face of the earth" where the white man had cleared the ground; Del Hardy felt "one of the pleasantest feelings a white man could have was, after tramping days in the everlasting forest, to come out on cleared land and look across open fields." True Son and Del Hardy see the same marks of white man's civilization, but they do not see them from the same points of view. What other facets of the white man's civilization do they see differently? How are these differences reflected in the words used to describe what they see?

2. What does Del think of True Son? What does he think of True Son's refusal to speak English to his white father? How does Aunt Kate react to the boy? Why?

3. What kind of woman is Myra Butler? How does she react to the son she has not seen for eleven years? How do you think the author wants the reader to feel about Myra Butler? Is that the way you feel? Why or why not?

4. Myra Butler tells her son, "Your education has been arrested. You've had to live in heathen darkness and ignorance." What point of view do those sentences reflect? How much does she know about Indian life? Cite sentences from the chapter to support your opinion.

5. According to his white mother, what is the most important thing for True Son to know? What is your reaction to her lesson?

6. Why does True Son resist being called John? Why does he stare "with loathing" at the pants and jacket?

7. Why do you think True Son is or is not a savage? Explain your answer.

Writing Assignment 1

Write a theme in which you take the position that one race is, or is not, superior to all others. Your task here is to give as many reasons as you can and to support your reasons with convincing evidence.

If you do not think one race is superior to all others, you should give as many reasons as you can to support your belief and you should offer evidence to support each of your reasons.

At the beginning of this chapter we raised some questions about how the color of a person's skin affects his perception of the world and how other people's perception of the person is, in turn, affected by his color and theirs. The excerpt from *The Light in the Forest* adds another dimension for you to consider as you attempt to answer questions about the effect of color upon point of view.

1. What race or "color" is True Son? Does his racial background "color" his point of view or not? If it does not, why doesn't it? What other factors are involved in his situation?
2. Look up the word *culture* in a dictionary and find a definition that might be relevant to your discussion of True Son's relationship to his white family and the white society. Is there a correlation between culture and color? How would you explain that relationship? Is True Son's situation unusual in terms of the relationship between his racial background and his cultural upbringing? Explain.

While you keep the results of this discussion in mind, read the following excerpt from "The Autobiography of an Ex-Coloured Man" by James Weldon Johnson. As you read, compare and contrast his experiences with those of True Son.

I Discover I Am a Negro

by James Weldon Johnson

1   My school-days ran along very pleasantly. I stood well in my studies, not always so well with regard to my behaviour. I was never guilty of any serious misconduct, but my love of fun sometimes got me into trouble. I remember, however, that my sense of humour was so sly that most of the trouble usually fell on the head of the other fellow. My ability to play on the piano at school exercises was looked upon as little short of marvellous in a boy of my age. I was not chummy with many of my mates, but, on the whole, was about as popular as it is good for a boy to be.

2   One day near the end of my second term at school the principal came into our room and, after talking to the teacher, for some reason said: "I wish all of the white scholars to stand for a moment." I rose with the others. The teacher looked at me and, calling my name, said: "You sit down for the present, and rise with the others." I did not quite understand her, and questioned: "Ma'm?" She repeated, with a softer tone in her voice: "You sit down now, and rise with the others." I sat down dazed. I saw and heard nothing. When the others were asked to rise, I did not know it. When school was dismissed, I went out in a kind of stupor. A few of the white boys jeered me, saying: "Oh, you're a nigger too." I heard some black children say: "We knew he was coloured." "Shiny" said to them: "Come along, don't tease him" and thereby won my undying gratitude.

3   I hurried on as fast as I could, and had gone some distance before I perceived that "Red Head" was walking by my side. After a while he said to me: "Le' me carry your books." I gave him my strap without being able to answer. When we got to my gate, he said as he handed me my books: "Say, you know my big red agate? I can't shoot with it any more. I'm going to bring it to school for you tomorrow." I took my books and ran into the house. As I passed through the hallway, I saw that my mother was busy with one of her customers; I rushed up into my own little room, shut the door, and went quickly to where my looking-glass hung on the wall. For an instant I was afraid to look, but when I did, I looked long and earnestly. I had often heard people say to my

mother: "What a pretty boy you have!" I was accustomed to hear remarks about my beauty; but now, for the first time, I became conscious of it and recognized it. I noticed the ivory whiteness of my skin, the beauty of my mouth, the size and liquid darkness of my eyes, and how the long, black lashes that fringed and shaded them produced an effect that was strangely fascinating even to me. I noticed the softness and glossiness of my dark hair that fell in waves over my temples, making my forehead appear whiter than it really was. How long I stood there gazing at my image I do not know. When I came out and reached the head of the stairs, I heard the lady who had been with my mother going out. I ran downstairs and rushed to where my mother was sitting, with a piece of work in her hands. I buried my head in her lap and blurted out: "Mother, tell me, am I a nigger?" I could not see her face, but I knew the piece of work dropped to the floor and I felt her hands on my head. I looked up into her face and repeated: "Tell me, mother, am I a nigger?" There were tears in her eyes and I could see that she was suffering for me. And then it was that I looked at her critically for the first time. I had thought of her in a childish way only as the most beautiful woman in the world; now I looked at her searching for defects. I could see that her skin was almost brown, that her hair was not so soft as mine, and that she did differ in some way from the other ladies who came to the house; yet, even so, I could see that she was very beautiful, more beautiful than any of them. She must have felt that I was examining her, for she hid her face in my hair and said with difficulty: "No, my darling, you are not a nigger." She went on: "You are as good as anybody; if anyone calls you a nigger, don't notice them." But the more she talked, the less was I reassured, and I stopped her by asking: "Well, mother, am I white? Are you white?" She answered tremblingly: "No, I am not white, but you— your father is one of the greatest men in the country— the best blood of the South is in you—" This suddenly opened up in my heart a fresh chasm of misgiving and fear, and I almost fiercely demanded: "Who is my father? Where is he?" She stroked my hair and said: "I'll tell you about him some day." I sobbed: "I want to know now." She answered: "No, not now."

4   Perhaps it had to be done, but I have never forgiven the woman who did it so cruelly. It may be that she never

knew that she gave me a sword-thrust that day in school which was years in healing.

Since I have grown older I have often gone back and tried to analyse the change that came into my life after that fateful day in school. There did come a radical change, and, young as I was, I felt fully conscious of it, though I did not fully comprehend it. Like my first spanking, it is one of the few incidents in my life that I can remember clearly. In the life of everyone there is a limited number of unhappy experiences which are not written upon the memory, but stamped there with a die; and in long years after, they can be called up in detail, and every emotion that was stirred by them can be lived through anew; these are the tragedies of life. We may grow to include some of them among the trivial incidents of childhood—a broken toy, a promise made to us which was not kept, a harsh, heart-piercing word—but these, too, as well as the bitter experiences and disappointments of mature years, are the tragedies of life.

5   And so I have often lived through that hour, that day, that week, in which was wrought the miracle of my transition from one world into another; for I did indeed pass into another world. From that time I looked out through other eyes, my thoughts were coloured, my words dictated, my actions limited by one dominating, all-pervading idea which constantly increased in force and weight until I finally realized in it a great, tangible fact.

And this is the dwarfing, warping, distorting influence which operates upon each and every coloured man in the United States. He is forced to take his outlook on all things, not from the view-point of a citizen, or a man, or even a human being, but from the view-point of a *coloured* man. It is wonderful to me that the race has progressed so broadly as it has, since most of its thought and all of its activity must run through the narrow neck of this one funnel.

And it is this, too, which makes the coloured people of this country, in reality, a mystery to the whites. It is a difficult thing for a white man to learn what a coloured man really thinks; because, generally, with the latter an additional and different light must be brought to bear on what he thinks; and his thoughts are often influenced by considerations so delicate and subtle that it would be impossible for him to confess or explain them to one of the opposite race. This gives to every coloured man, in proportion to his intellectuality, a sort of dual personality; there is one phase of him which is disclosed only in the freemasonry of his own race. I have often watched with interest and sometimes with amazement even ignorant coloured men under cover of broad grins and minstrel antics maintain this dualism in the presence of white men.

6   I believe it to be a fact that the coloured people of this country know and understand the white people better than the white people know and understand them.

I now think that this change which came into my life was at first more subjective than objective. I do not think my friends at school changed so much toward me as I did toward them. I grew reserved, I might say suspicious. I grew constantly more and more afraid of laying myself open to some injury to my feelings or my pride. I frequently saw or fancied some slight where, I am sure, none was intended. On the other hand, my friends and teachers were, if anything different, more considerate of me; but I can remember that it was against this very attitude in particular that my sensitiveness revolted. "Red" was the only one who did not so wound me; up to this day I recall with a swelling heart his clumsy efforts to make me understand that nothing could change his love for me.

7   I am sure that at this time the majority of my white schoolmates did not understand or appreciate any differences between me and themselves; but there were a few who had evidently received instructions at home on the matter, and more than once they displayed their knowledge in word and action. As the years passed, I noticed that the most innocent and ignorant among the others grew in wisdom.

8   I myself would not have so clearly understood this difference had it not been for the presence of the other coloured children at school; I had learned what their status was, and now I learned that theirs was mine. I had had no particular like or dislike for these black and brown boys and girls; in fact, with the exception of "Shiny," they had occupied very little of my thought; but I do know that when the blow fell, I had a very strong aversion to being classed with them. So I became something of a solitary. "Red" and I remained inseparable, and there was between "Shiny" and me a sort of sympathetic bond, but my intercourse with the others

was never entirely free from a feeling of constraint. I must add, however, that this feeling was confined almost entirely to my intercourse with boys and girls of about my own age; I did not experience it with my seniors. And when I grew to manhood, I found myself freer with elderly white people than with those near my own age.

9   I was now about eleven years old, but these emotions and impressions which I have just described could not have been stronger or more distinct at an older age. There were two immediate results of my forced loneliness: I began to find company in books, and greater pleasure in music. . . .

Discussion

As you discuss the incident related by Mr. Johnson, you might want to explore the answers to questions such as the following:

1. How is Mr. Johnson's real-life situation similar to True Son's? How is it different?
2. Do you think that the actual differences between Johnson and his classmates were greater or less than those between True Son and his white family? In what ways is True Son different from his white family and Del? In what ways is Johnson different from "Red Head" and the rest of his white classmates?
3. How do the white men perceive True Son to be different from them? In what ways does he perceive himself to be different from them? In what ways is Johnson perceived to be different by his classmates? Does that perception change during the incident related? In what ways does Johnson perceive himself to be different from his classmates? Does his perception change during the incident related? How and why?
4. In the first paragraph of section 5, Mr. Johnson says that he "indeed pass[ed] into another world" after the incident he describes. How would you compare this experience with True Son's experience?
5. How do you respond to the incident related by Mr. Johnson? How do you respond to him as a person? as a writer? Does your race or color affect that response? How does your response compare with the responses of some of your

classmates? Does there seem to be a correlation between each student's color and his response, or is it difficult to see any specific correlation?

6. Reread the first paragraph of section 7. What do you think are the differences between the writer and his white schoolmates? Do you agree that most of them were not aware of the differences? Support your opinion. What do you think the writer means when he says "a few ... had evidently received instructions at home on the matter"? In what specific ways do you think they displayed this instruction?

Does this suggest that the way people respond to "color" can actually create cultural differences between races who might otherwise share most aspects of the same culture? Does this suggest, in other words, that people of different races can become culturally different when large numbers of one or both races perceive of themselves and of each other as different? If so, might it not be that members of different races develop or nurture cultural traits distinctively their own so that the differences between the races, largely imagined and exaggerated at first, become more actual the longer the original "myth" is held and perpetuated? (Again it might be useful to contrast this situation with True Son's situation.)

7. How do you respond to section 8 of the excerpt? Why?

8. At the end of the selection you learn that the writer was "about eleven years old" at the time he discovered he was a Negro. Do you find this difficult to believe? What in the selection helps to make this believable?

Writing Assignment 2

Imagine that you are writing your autobiography. Try to remember the first time you were made aware of color or race. If you cannot recall the first time, think of an incident in your life in which race or color was a significant factor. Recreate the incident as carefully, vividly, and accurately as you can, trying to relate your feelings at the time, as well as why you reacted as you did. Don't tell the reader how you would react now, if you think that reaction would be different. Explain how it was at the time. Remember that you are writing an autobiographical account; therefore it should be as accurate and honest as you can make it, even if doing so may cause you some discomfort.

Writing Assignment 3

John O. Killens, a black writer, in an article entitled "We Refuse to Look at Ourselves Through the Eyes of White America," writes:

> All men react to life through man-made symbols. Even our symbolic reactions are different from yours. To give a few examples:
>
> In the center of a little Southern town near the border of Mississippi, there is a water tower atop which is a large white cross, illumined at night with a lovely (awesome to Negroes) neoned brightness. It can be seen for many miles away. To most white Americans who see it for the first time it is a beacon light that symbolizes the Cross upon which Jesus died, and it gives them a warm feeling in the face and shoulders. But the same view puts an angry knot in the black man's belly. To him it symbolizes the very, very "Christian" K.K.K.[1]
>
> To the average white man, a courthouse, even in Mississippi, is a place where justice is dispensed. To me, the black man, it is a place where justice is dispensed—with.
>
> Even our white hero symbols are different from yours. You give us moody Abraham Lincoln, but many of us prefer John Brown, whom most of you hold in contempt and regard as a fanatic; meaning, of course, that the firm dedication of any white man to the freedom of the black man is a *prima facie* evidence of perversion and insanity.

As a class, discuss Mr. Killens' comments, and see if you can think of any other symbols that whites and blacks are likely to react to in different ways. Remember that symbols can be words (patriotism), pictures (a typical Norman Rockwell cover) or clothing (a soldier's uniform) or virtually anything else in a particular context.

After your discussion, write a short story or a play that portrays how one's color or race can cause him to react a

[1] *K.K.K.*: Ku Klux Klan.

particular way to a particular symbol or symbols. You can use a personal experience as the basis for your story or play, or you can make something up. (The selections you have read in this section should give you some ideas.)

If you choose, you can write an essay instead of a story or play, in which you discuss the relationship between race and symbols. If you disagree with Mr. Killens, you may show why, giving support for your position with specific examples. If you agree, you should give further examples and support for the idea.

Writing Assignment 4

In a letter to the editor of a daily newspaper, a woman wrote: "I believe, like the Hebrew nation that wandered in the wilderness until the doubters fell by the wayside, that our young people can lead us out of this dilemma of prejudice and hate."

That sentence echoes the sentiments of thousands of people who believe that prejudice and hate will diminish in the future. But how?

Your writing task is to prepare a plan for overcoming racial prejudice. The people to whom you will present your plan—your classmates, the school board, the citizens in your community, or the entire population of the United States or of the world—will be your audience.

How would you go about organizing people to help? Would you rely solely upon the young "to lead us out of this dilemma of prejudice and hate," or would you also involve members of older generations? How would you involve them? What would you do in the schools? In the churches? In government? In the home? Would you pass laws designed to end prejudice or would you use other means? What other means?

If you would rather not become involved in such a plan, or if you believe that nothing can be done to end racial prejudice, write a theme in which you present this point of view.

Chapter 8

People, Religions, and Issues

People believe. Whether they believe in one god, many gods, or no gods, they believe in something or someone. What they believe shapes their responses to other people, to events, to politics—to everything. What they believe can make them tolerant or intolerant, for when they commit themselves entirely to some belief, they tend to accept, ignore, or discard other ideas according to their beliefs.

A person's religious beliefs can cause him to look at many things—not just God and sin, which you would expect—from a specific point of view. For example, when five religious leaders who all call themselves Protestants were asked by a Catholic priest to respond to the topic "Human Nature, Corrupt or Noble?" each wrote a response that reflected his religious point of view. The responses of three of the five theologians are reprinted here without identifying the writers or their faiths.

Human Nature, Corrupt or Noble?

I

Human nature is depraved and debased. God made man in his own image, but sin came to destroy the image. The natural man cannot even comprehend the things of God—"They are foolishness unto him: neither can he know them, because they are spiritually discerned" (1 Cor 2:14). "Flesh and blood cannot inherit the kingdom of God" (1 Cor 15:50). A man must be born again by faith in Jesus Christ. He must receive a new nature. Ezekiel, speaking for God, says, "I will take the stony heart out of their flesh, and will give them an heart of flesh" (Ezek 11:19).

Some years ago I went with a group of Greek Christians for a little time of fellowship and prayer together on Mars Hill at Athens. I looked up to the Acropolis. There stands the Parthenon, one of the loveliest buildings ever built by man. It is a ruin now—its carvings removed, its wall broken, its roof gone. But as I saw it that day, the colors of a sunset sky were reflected in the chipped stone and ruined pediment. I forgot for a moment I was looking at a ruin; and I received at least a vague impression of what the building must have looked like in its pristine beauty, fresh from the hands of its builder. Under the right circumstances when "the light is right," so to speak, I can still see in fallen human nature a faint suggestion of the image of God wherein man was originally created. But sin has wrecked the image. The Temple is fallen into decay, and only an act of divine rebuilding—that miracle of regeneration which we call the New Birth—can restore that Temple.

II

Sin did not destroy human nature. If it had, then God could not have become man to save us from our sin, for God then would have had to become a sinner. Moreover, if sin were basic to human nature, then human beings could never enter heaven, for the removal of their sinfulness by Christ's work on the cross would be the removal of themselves!

Contemporary existentialist theologians, as well as those, like Tillich,[1] who have been much influenced by existentialism,[2] have gotten into this kind of pickle by asserting that man falls "from essence to existence"— that Creation and Fall are really coterminous and equally necessary to the definition of man.

Actually, sinfulness is not the product of man's

[1] *Paul Johannes Tillich,* German-born American teacher of theology, who believes that the great religious questions deal with being, existence, and life and that no human truth is ultimate.
[2] *Existentialism,* a philosophy stating that man is free from control by God or by a fixed human nature and that thus man is entirely responsible for what he makes of himself.

nature; it is the result of man's freely chosen misuse of his nature. God created man with free will, with the high privilege of choosing to serve God or to serve himself. As C. S. Lewis so effectively argued, love cannot be forced, and it must always accept the possibility of rejection. God, who is love, gave His creatures the choice of loving Him or not, and they, in choosing to be free of God, fell into a bondage of the most absolute kind. Said Jesus: "Truly, truly, I say to you, every one who commits sin is a slave to sin" (Jn 8:33–34). This bondage so conditions each subsequent generation that the choices open to the children of sinners become sinful choices within an already sinful context—and the race wanders in a labyrinth that has (humanly speaking, in Sartre's [3] words), "no exit." The children of Adam have the freedom to choose their own poison, but not to perform curative operations on themselves. Only the Great Physician—Jesus Christ, who "was in all points tempted like as we are, yet without sin" (Heb 4:15)—can provide the remedy we need, for only He did not succumb to the disease. And in not succumbing, He displays what human nature properly is, and shows men the noble potentiality which God can actualize when sin's drag-effect is removed.

III

The tragic, intractable character of human nature seems to me to be true and was appropriately rediscovered by American theology in the 30's and the 40's, given our experience of depression and war. Today we must build on the rediscovery of the tragic element of life. We must build on the so-called pessimism of the new orthodoxy revival and notice that life has another element too: men can in fact make decisions that count, and the newer technologies, far from being merely depersonalizing as traditional critics of technology like Erich Fromm [1] and Herbert Marcuse [2] and Paul Tillich

[3] *Jean Paul Sartre*, French existential philosopher who in 1944 wrote a play entitled *No Exit*.
[1] *Erich Fromm*, German-born American psychoanalyst and author (*The Sane Society, The Art of Loving*) who believes that man in our industrial society has become estranged from himself.
[2] *Herbert Marcuse*, German-born American philosopher and author (*One-Dimensional Man, Eros and Civilization*) whose concepts of manipulation and control of man by government have been taken up by the New Left.

have said, are in fact technologies that enable our decisions to count. Therefore there is a case not for the nobility of human nature, but for a more modest optimism about both personal and historical possibilities today.

The same three Protestant theologians were asked to comment on communism. Here are their responses:

Christianity and Communism

I

Christianity puts an imprimatur [1] on no economic or political system. Neither capitalism nor communism, neither oligarchy nor democracy is "God's system." We do the gospel a great disservice when we uncritically identify it with "the stars and stripes forever"—with our "American way of life."

"Communism" (communal ownership of wealth) is thus not to be condemned *per se* by Christianity. But atheism is, and so is totalitarianism (the subjugation of all life and values to the state). Insofar as Russian or Chinese communism is atheistic and totalitarian, *to that extent* and *for those reasons* it must be rejected as demonic. But *if* (and it is a big if, admittedly) the Russian state continues to exert less and less totalitarian pressure on its people, and *if* Marxist theoreticians like Garaudy were to succeed in convincing the party that atheism is not a necessary base for community ideology, then Christians would have no legitimate *theological* ground for blasting Russian communism. Hochhuth's play *The Deputy* (whatever we may think of its portrait of Pius XII), points up the terrible danger of viewing communism as the worst of all evils, thereby allowing the end to justify the means in opposing it—with the result that even greater evils are perpetrated.

Furthermore, there is something more than a little disquieting in Jesus' teachings about not picking out specks in other people's eyes before extracting beams from one's own. Why, therefore, don't we American Christians devote some time to cleaning up our own capitalistic mess, where self-centered management tries

[1] *imprimatur:* stamp of approval.

to run roughshod over government (remember the issue of steel prices?), where self-centered and corrupt labor leaders try to make everyone knuckle-under, even in time of war (Jimmie Hoffa inevitably comes to mind), and where all of us in a fat-cat economy justify our fat cathood in terms of individual initiative, while much of the world's population goes to bed hungry.

II

Communism is a Satanic force. It is from the Eastern Communist bloc that the armies will come up against Jerusalem in an effort to destroy God's people Israel "that dwell safely" in the land (Ezek 38:11). A free nation, a democracy, either must oppose Communism or be destroyed by it. We should clean out the Communist sympathizers in our government and remove the men who are "soft" toward Communism, some of whom seem even to have come to cabinet rank. Private ownership of property is approved in Scripture. One of the situations that will exist under the millennial reign of Christ is that every man shall sit under his vine and his fig tree, and no man shall make him afraid (Micah 4:4).

III

It seems to me that the only thing necessary to say here is that there is no danger of communism in the North American continent today. What we need to enable ourselves and our young people today to survive in the future is more effective encounter with and dialogue with communism as an ideology. This is what European, African, and Asian students get naturally, and we shelter our children, our young people, and even our college students from this. Anyone who does not know the power of communism from the inside cannot really be an effective citizen, either intellectually or practically.

Discussion

1. How much agreement is there among the three theologians on the topic, "Human Nature, Corrupt or Noble"? On which points do they agree? On which points do they differ?

With which writer do you agree most? Why? With which writer do you disagree most? Why?

2. With which response to communism do you agree most? Why? With which writer do you disagree most? Why? How do your religious beliefs influence your attitude toward communism?

3. In *Spectrum of Protestant Beliefs*, the book in which the comments on human nature and communism appear, the editor, a Catholic priest, says that the three contributors represent these views of Protestantism: fundamentalism, confessionalism, and radicalism. After reading the editor's descriptions of each of those attitudes toward Protestantism, decide which of the comments on human nature and communism were written by the fundamentalist, the confessionalist, and the radical. What reasons can you give for your decisions? Compare your choices and your reasons with those of your classmates. How do the reasons differ? Why do they differ?

Three Views of Christianity

Fundamentalist

The fundamentalist is characterized by a great devotion to the Bible and its inerrancy,[1] by orthodoxy concerning basic Christian doctrines, and a conviction that salvation is by faith alone. He rejects all biblical criticism, and a literal interpretation of Scripture leads him to deny the theory of evolution. He has a strong belief in the traditional Christian teaching about heaven and hell, the divinity of Jesus Christ, the Trinity, Virgin Birth of Jesus, his atoning death on the cross, his Resurrection and Ascension into heaven.... Fundamentalists also stress the Second Coming of Jesus Christ, preach it frequently, and many consider this return to be imminent.

Fundamentalists lay great emphasis on salvation by faith alone. Once a man has accepted Jesus Christ as his personal Savior, he is regenerated, born again, saved. Good works do not help toward salvation, but the man who has sincere faith will live a good life. Salvation is accomplished here and now, and the good works follow

[1] *inerrancy:* infallibility.

as a result, not *vice versa* as the Catholic and Orthodox and some Protestant groups teach.

Confessional

Contrasting to the "We have no creed but the gospel" attitude of the fundamentalists is the concern shown by "high church" Episcopalians and some Lutherans, notably Missouri Synod, for close adherence to a "confession of faith." The authoritative statement of church doctrine in the Apostles' Creed or Nicene Creed or in their own denominational confession of faith is considered by them to be the safest guide to the basic message of the Bible. This tradition considers the ecclesiastical organization to be a thing of much more authority and importance than do the fundamentalists or new evangelicals. In the latter two groups, congregations are more likely to be autonomous than among the ecclesiastically-oriented confessional group.

Doctrinally, confessional Protestants cover the spectrum from center to right: some are highly orthodox, accepting such key points of high orthodoxy as the reality of Satan and the Second Coming of Christ; others question this or that traditional doctrine, and some verge on a rejection of the physical reality of the Virgin Birth of Christ. Rejection of this would locate a person in the liberal camp.

Politically, the confessional person might be anywhere on the spectrum, but probably the majority tend to be conservative.

Radical

The radical challenges the existence of God as a personal being, one who can know and will. "God is dead" and "Christian atheism" are the radical's slogans. He claims to be a Christian, faithful to the humanitarian values preached by Christ, and looking to Christ as the supreme expression of perfect humanity. He rejects any idea of a supernatural being, rejects also the organized church as an anachronism. All traditional Christian doctrines are for him "irrelevant to the life of modern man." On the extreme religious left, the radical usually is on the political left, too.

Discussion

1. Given the hypothetical possibility that a group of one hundred children were placed at infancy in a setting where there were no adult human beings, how, according to the views expressed by each of the theologians, would the children behave? (You must assume, of course, that there would be some way of caring for their needs and wants during infancy. Don't let this problem enter into the hypothetical situation, just consider the theological questions.) According to each view, how would the children be likely to act and why? What kind of society would they be likely to build? How would they be likely to behave toward each other? toward God? toward various activities that are likely to evolve? Answer the questions as you think each theologian would answer them, giving support from the comments you have from each about human nature.

2. Given this same situation, what kind of economic and political system would be likely to evolve from this group, looking at it from the point of view of each theologian? Why? Support each hypothesis by referring to the ideas each man expresses about communism.

3. If such a situation were possible, how do *you* think it would turn out? What kind of adults would the children turn out to be? What kind of social, economic, political systems would they be likely to develop? Look at these questions from your own theological position.

Writing Assignment 1

Do your religious beliefs (or lack of them) ever influence the way you behave toward your friends or family? Do your religious beliefs ever enter into your decision to join a certain group or attend a specific event?

Describe an incident in which your religious beliefs caused you to behave in a certain way or to react to others in a certain manner. If you cannot think of an incident, try to imagine one in which religious beliefs would influence what you think or say.

Following are a few questions that might help you focus

on an incident and think more clearly about it before you attempt to describe it in writing:

1. Have I ever said something to a friend or member of my family because of my religious beliefs? What was it? Why did I say it? Did he understand why I said what I did? How did he or she react? What happened?
2. Did I ever refuse to attend an event because of my beliefs? Why did I refuse? To whom did I refuse? Did the other person or persons involved understand the reason for my refusal? Did they accept my reasons, or did I offer any? Why or why not?
3. Did I ever say anything to a person that offended him because of his beliefs or lack of them? What did I say? Why did it offend him? What happened? What did I learn from the incident?

Your purpose here is to describe an incident so well that your reader, a person your own age, will be able to visualize exactly what happened and understand why it happened. Your purpose is not to prove that you were *right* in doing or saying what you did. Rather, your purpose is to describe the incident so well that your reader will understand exactly what happened and will know why you said or did what you did.

Writing Assignment 2

Do you know what members of various faiths believe? What do you know about the various denominations of Protestantism? about Judaism? about Catholicism? about Islam? about Buddhism?

Read about a religion that interests you but that you know little about. Find out the basic beliefs of the members of that religion. What do they believe? Why?

After carefully studying several books and/or articles on that religion, write a paper in which you (1) explain the fundamental beliefs of the religion and (2) compare those beliefs with your own. How are they similar? How do they differ? Why do they differ?

Chapter 9

You,
Your Language,
and
Your Writing Voice

A LOOK IN THE MIRROR

The words you say and how you say them can reveal a great deal about your personality. Just as clothes are said to "make" the man or woman, your language tends to make you what you are. In other words, your language *is* you.

Perhaps you have never thought of your language as reflecting the "true you." You may never have thought of your language as being "you" at all. But it might be worthwhile to consider both your clothing and your language as reflections of yourself.

Your answers to the following questions might help you understand what your clothing can reveal about you.

1. What kind of clothes do I like? Why? What do they tell other people about me?
2. What kind of clothes do I wear to school? Why do they or don't they reveal anything about my character?
3. Do I prefer bright colors or subdued colors? What does my taste in colors reveal about my personality?

4. If I like bright colors, do I sometimes wear duller ones on specific occasions? When? Why? What do my choice of clothing and choice of colors on specific occasions tell another person about me?
5. Do my clothes reveal anything about my economic condition? about my religious beliefs? about my view of my physical self? about my race? about my view of society?
6. Do I ever wear ornaments, costume jewelry, a watch, or anything else that is not absolutely necessary to keep me clothed and warm (or cool, depending on the season)? Why do I wear ornaments? What do they reveal about me?
7. Do I ever wear ornaments that are symbols of what I believe, such as a cross, a Star of David, a peace symbol, a political button? What do I want that symbol to tell others about me?

What Message Are You Sending?

Our language is a kind of clothing that we wrap around our thoughts, emotions, and desires before we present them to other people. *What* we say is very important when we try to communicate with people. But *how* we say it is equally important. Sometimes, the actual message that we send to listeners or readers is not as important as the words we use to convey the message. For example, if a younger brother or sister wants to play and you're busy, you might say:

"I can't play right now. Maybe later."

Or you might say:

"Get out of here, you little bum. Can't you see I'm busy?"

The message is essentially the same: you can't play now. But consider the impact of the words in both messages on the younger brother or sister. What will he or she think about you? What has your language told him or her about you?

If we put the wrong clothes on our thoughts, people might not listen to what we have to say. How we convey our message may offend or displease our listeners or readers in some way. Of course, the opposite can also be true. If we put the right clothes on what we have to say, some people will listen to us even if they don't agree with our message.

Discussion

1. Do I ever think consciously about the words I use? When? Why?
2. Do I change my language for different occasions? Why, or why not? How do I change it?
3. Do people make judgments about me based on the way I talk or write? Do I make judgments about others based on their language? What kinds of judgments are these likely to be?
4. To what am I more likely to respond when I meet a new person—his clothes or his language? Why?
5. Am I more conscious of what a person says than I am of how he says it?
6. When meeting new people, am I more conscious of how I look or how I sound to them? Does this vary with the situation? How and why?

A DIFFERENT MEDIUM

Talking is such a common everyday experience for virtually all of us that we seldom think about it. How often do you listen to yourself when you speak? Most of us will probably have to say "not very often." This is not unusual or surprising since most of our daily conversation is taken up with what might be called the pots and pans of daily existence: asking for the salt, asking directions, exchanging ritual greetings— "hello, how are you . . . ," answering questions to which the answers are already known, and so on.

When we write, it is usually a different matter. Then, our statements are not likely to be so automatic, so casual, so unconsciously formed and expressed. Most of us are a little more hesitant and conscious about our written responses than we are about our spoken ones. Writing, by its very nature, is, or at least should be, a process of discovery—a process that makes us more consciously aware of what we say, and how and why we have said it. This process can also make us more aware of who we are and why we are as we are.

Writing takes more time than speaking; hence, it gives us more time to think about what we are going to say. It also gives us a chance to go back and look at what we have said to see if it is what we meant to say. Not only does writing give us an opportunity to do all of these things, it *requires* us to do them. If we do not, it is very possible that we will not say what we mean to say, not say what we have to say clearly enough for the reader to understand it, or simply not say anything worth saying.

When we talk, our audience is normally present. The audience not only hears the words we speak; but it also can hear the tone, the pitch, the inflection, and the volume of our voice as we say words. In addition, an audience can watch our facial expressions and our gestures. All of these things can say as much or more than the words themselves. In fact, they can make the same words say totally different things. Look at the short, simple, typical dialogue which follows; read it silently, and think about what it means. You might feel it is so obvious that there is no need to think about it, but think about what it might *imply* about what it does not actually say.

He: Hi, how are you?

She: Oh, I'm fine. How are you?

He: Oh, I'm just great. It sure is good to see you. How was your summer?

She: Yeah, good to see you, too. Well, you know how summers are with the old folks at home. I'm really glad to be back. How about yourself?

He: Yeah.

She: Well, I got to run now. Will I be seeing you around?

He: Yeah, I guess so. Take it easy.

She: Bye.

He: Yeah, see ya.

Have three pairs of students dramatize the dialogue according to the way they think the words ought to be spoken to convey what they believe the words actually mean. (The second and third pairs of students should remain out of the room while the first pair presents their dramatic interpretation, and so on. If possible, each dramatization should be tape recorded so that the class can hear it again.) As you listen, jot down what you think is going on between the two people.

After you have heard all three dramatizations, decide if each pair has or has not conveyed the same message.

1. Was there anything suggested about the relationship between the boy and girl in any or all of the dramatizations? What was suggested and how? Were different relationships suggested by the various interpretations?
2. How did intonation and inflection convey information? What information did it convey?
3. Did any of the actors use gestures? What were they? What did they convey to you?

This simple dialogue and dramatization should suggest some of the interesting aspects of verbal communication, even at the simplest level. It might also allow us to contemplate what happens when we try to translate oral language into written language.

Since the dialogue was written, the actors had to interpret it as they spoke it. Were they given any clues as to how to speak the lines? Could the writer of these lines have given the speakers more help as to how the lines should be spoken?

If you were translating one (or all three) of the oral interpretations into writing, how would you do it? What would you have to add to help the reader understand the relationship between the two speakers? How do you translate tone and inflection into writing?

WRITING FOR AN AUDIENCE

There are other things to think about as you investigate the differences between spoken and written communication. When members of your audience are present, they can and usually do give you constant and immediate feedback. They stop you with their own comments, they ask questions, they nod assent, they say no, they look confused, they look bored, they smile. They do countless things that explicitly or implicitly give you information about how well and how accurately they are receiving your message. If you ask for salt and they pass it, you know you have achieved your purpose.

If you are expounding on your own wisdom or beauty and your audience walks out or turns on the T.V., you recognize that you are not communicating or are communicating the wrong thing.

But what is the case when you write? Where is your audience and how do they let you know if you are communicating with them?

The truth is, you seldom see your audience and, in fact, may not even know any, or many of them, personally. Needless to say, this places great demands upon you if you want your purpose in writing to be achieved—to be read and understood.

Even though an awareness of audience is essential for most writing, most inexperienced writers fail because they give little or no thought to their audience. They address their audience in writing as if they were speaking to them in person. But writing demands more of you than speaking. Honest writing forces you to think more deeply about a topic and explain it more clearly than informal speaking does. How many times have you read something, even a letter from a friend, and wished that the writer were there so you could ask him what in the world he was talking about? When you speak, especially to people you know, you can use a kind of shorthand or code language because you usually talk about experiences you have shared with listeners. But in writing you do not always know what experiences your audience has had.

Writing Assignment 1

Think about the conversations in the lunch room or in rap sessions. Sometimes they are filled with partially developed allusions to the day's events, with inside jokes in which a single word expresses an entire idea, with slang words that call to mind a whole series of shared experiences, and with a phrase or gesture that evokes a series of mutual responses. Sometimes nothing needs to be said or done to communicate a great deal.

Listen carefully to the next two or three conversations among friends. Take the role of an outsider, a "new kid," and try to discover how much of what is said would be understandable if you did not know the people involved and the things they are talking about in a kind of code language.

Prepare a script for a skit or write a short story in which you are the outsider trying to get into a conversation. How do you feel? How do you attempt to join the conversation? What happens? Do you say the wrong things? Why? Do you know the reasons for the laughter? Do you laugh at the wrong time? Why?

If you prefer to dramatize the situation, how can you convey to the audience how the stranger in the group feels? What directions will you give to the actors? How will you convey embarrassment or bewilderment through dialogue?

If you write a short story, what will the reader learn about the stranger's thoughts? What technique will you use to help the reader find out what the stranger thinks? How does the stranger act? What does he say? Why? Will your reader be able to determine the answers to these questions as he reads your story?

Your task is to dramatize, either in a skit or a short story, a conversation in which you are a stranger in a group. Your purpose is to convey to the audience—your classmates—your frustrations as you attempt to join the conversation. Your readers, or the audience for your skit, should be able to detect just how much of the conversation and the accompanying gestures the stranger correctly interprets and how much he misinterprets.

Writing Assignment 2

If you have completed most of the writing assignments in this book, you have written for different audiences. But how do you decide how to write for different groups? Are there ways of assessing an audience?

To help you answer these questions, you might try this experiment. Select a household appliance, part of a car, a simple model of an airplane or car, or a simple dress pattern and explain orally how it works to the following four people:

a child between the ages of six and nine

a person your own age and sex

a person your own age of the opposite sex

an adult

Did you use the same vocabulary for all four people? If not, what were the differences? What adjustments did you have to make for each audience? How precise did your instructions have to be?

After you have given the instructions orally, select one person and write a set of instructions for him or her. Now what do you have to take into consideration? How do the written instructions differ from the oral ones? Why do they differ?

After writing your instructions, give them to one of those to whom you gave the instructions orally. Can he or she understand them? If not, why do you think the person failed? What do you need to do to help him or her follow your directions?

THE VOICE YOU PROJECT

When you communicate through writing, your language is indeed you. There is no face, no spoken voice, no gesture—nothing but written words on a piece of paper.

What sort of person do you convey to your readers when you write? Look at some of the papers you have previously written in English class or elsewhere and attempt to read them as objectively as possible, asking yourself what sort of person lies behind the voice conveyed by the words on the page. Is there a voice at all? Does it sound like a real person? Does it sound like me? Was I deliberately trying to sound a particular way when I wrote the paper, or does all of my writing seem to sound the same way? Is that good? Why or why not?

Read some of the papers of your classmates, asking the same set of questions. If you didn't know who wrote the paper, could you connect it with the author? Why or why not?

People tend to reveal themselves—frequently, more than they might realize—in letters to the editors of newspapers. Have your class read the letters in your local newspaper for about a week and discuss what impressions you get of their writers. What specifically causes your impressions? How accurate do you think they are? Why do you think most of the writers are or are not conscious of the fact that they convey a personality to the reader through their writing?

By now it should be obvious that every time we talk or write about anything, we also say something about ourselves.

Every one of us is both unique and complex. We are unlike all other people in many different ways, and we are really not one person—but many. Who we are varies with the time, the place, the situation, and so forth. The problem for us as writers, then, is not to present the same voice or person every time we write, but to select an appropriate voice for the particular purpose and audience for which we are writing. All too often our writing voice is inappropriate or false. Writing of this kind is seldom effective even if it has a great deal to say. The reader will simply be turned off or bored when the writer's voice seems phony or more like a machine than a real person.

To get a better idea of different writing voices, look at different books, articles, and newspaper stories that deal with one topic that interests you. If you are interested in history, for example, pick a particular event and compare how it is handled in your history text, other history books, biographical accounts, magazine articles, and so on. As you read, answer the following questions:

1. In what significant ways do the accounts differ?
2. How does the language in the various accounts differ? Does it differ because of the author's point of view, or because of his purpose, or because of other factors? What other factors significantly affect the language of each author?
3. Which of the accounts seems most accurate? Why? Which seems most objective? Most subjective? Why? What specific examples can I cite to support my opinion?
4. Which of the accounts do I like best? Why? Does each author convey a distinctive voice? Do I have some idea of what they are like? Do some tell me more about themselves than others? How? Do some writers remain quite unknown to me even though their words seem real, human and interesting? Can I determine why by comparing the accounts?

Writing Assignment 3

Select an incident from your own past or an event from history that you can retell from the following three points of view:

> a historian who tries to write an objective, accurate account of the event from various sources

a biographer who is more interested in making the people in the historical event seem special and exciting than in adhering strictly to the known facts

a writer of fiction who uses the historical event as the basis of a novel or short story

As writers, we do not have complete control over the topic or subject matter we are writing about. Our control ends when we submit our writing to an audience. At that point they begin to shape and interpret what we have written from their own points of view and according to their own experiences. This is inevitable, and as writers, we must recognize that it must, and will, happen. That recognition will help us to write with our audience in mind, making certain that we have done everything possible to make what we have said—and why we have said it—as clear and forceful as possible. If the reader then misinterprets, it is probably because of his own carelessness, inability or unwillingness to confront the writing on its own terms, and to suspend his own preconceptions until he has read what the writer has to say.

The whole process becomes very complex, as it must necessarily be, in order to get at the truth. The "truth" will often depend upon what you are trying to do with the materials you are working with and how effective you are in making your readers aware of your intent. If you are pretending to write history but are really writing fiction, you are being dishonest. If you are writing history but your readers think you are writing fiction, you are being ineffective. If you are writing history, however, and realize that you can never know the whole truth, but can only attempt to approximate it as accurately as possible, you are conveying a legitimate point of view.

Chapter 10

The Roles You Play

You play roles every day: they may not be as diverse and distinct as those you assumed for the writing tasks in the last chapter; you are probably seldom so aware of changing roles as you were while dealing with Writing Assignment 3. But you, like all of us, play many roles just getting through an ordinary day.

This idea may strike some of you as foolish or offensive. It might seem foolish because you may seldom think of yourself as playing a role. You merely do what you do; you are what you are. The things that you say and do each day come easily and spontaneously. You don't have to think about being Frank or Connie or Tim or Mary, for example, because that is who you are. On the other hand, the idea of role-playing as a normal activity might strike you as offensive, because you might look upon anyone who plays different roles as a phony, asking yourself: "Who does he think he is? Why does he always have to be playing some kind of role?"

Discussion

1. Do I agree that all people play different roles while pursuing the activities of a normal day? Why or why not?
2. Why do I think of some people, usually ones I do not like, as "playing roles?" Are they the only ones who do this? If so, is that why I find them offensive? If I think all people play roles, why is it that I am only aware of it or offended by it with some people?
3. What kind of roles do I play? How do the roles affect my

actions, my responses, my emotions, my language? Why do I find some roles more comfortable than others?

4. Am I always, or ever, aware of playing a role? Am I sometimes aware of it? When? Why? How do such situations differ from ones in which I am not aware of being a role-player?

ACTORS AND THEIR ROLES

When we go to a movie, we may laugh or cry even though we know that what we are seeing is not "real" life. The actors are acting. Yet, even so the distinction between the actor and his role is sometimes blurred or forgotten. In the minds of many of his fans, an actor and his role may become quite inseparable.

Think of John Wayne without a cowboy hat or a horse, Lee Marvin as a kindly doctor, Dustin Hoffman as John Wayne, or Elizabeth Taylor as the Flying Nun. There are hundreds of instances of viewers becoming so involved with the daytime serials or soap operas that they write not to the actors but to the characters they play. If a favorite character is written out of a series because an actor is leaving, irate letters will come in protesting the character's absence. If the actor then shows up somewhere else in a different role, the shock to some viewers is as traumatic as it would be if a relative had returned from the dead in the guise of a different person.

Perhaps such responses can be interpreted as a high compliment to the actor's ability in portraying a character, but they also illustrate something important about real life—that most of us only think about people playing roles when they play them badly or unnaturally, when they attempt to be something or someone they are not. In our real roles, we are natural and professional. Like our shoes, our roles are seldom noticeable to us unless they are new or uncomfortable.

A writer must play a role. For many of us the role of writer is unfamiliar—even unnatural. Frequently this unfamiliarity results in a voice that makes the writer sound like someone he is not: the voice he projects does not result—as it should—from the deliberate choice of a suitable role. He is, to put it very simply, failing—on paper, at least—to be the person he wants to be.

It is only after we become comfortable in our role as a writer that we quit acting, that we discover and develop our own voice and personality and learn how to project ourselves in writing. The role becomes natural; a piece of paper no longer causes stage fright or self-conscious posturing. Like the seasoned actor, we assume the role with a minimum of difficulty and a maximum of efficiency. When this happens, we can shift roles as a writer the same way we do as we move through our everyday affairs.

Usually, it is only when we must assume a new or unfamiliar role that we temporarily become conscious of it. As soon as the role becomes familiar, we no longer think about it and it becomes part of our normal repertoire. Part of growing up is the assumption of an increasing number of roles, the loss of others, and the ability to accept and function in many roles. However, rather than being distinct and unrelated roles, most of them are supporting and complimentary, with one fading and merging into the next like the various scenes in a film.

What Roles Do You Play?

You have been a student now for some years, and while you may not always like the role or play it to the satisfaction of your parents or your teachers, you do know the ins and outs of it thoroughly. For you, it is not a difficult role to play adequately even though you may not win any academy awards. Most likely you do not think of it as a "role," but merely as one of the things you normally do.

Think about, and then list on a sheet of paper, all of the things you do in a typical week that require you to perform in a slightly or almost completely different way than you do as a student. Ask yourself the following questions:

1. What roles do I play at home?
2. If I work, what does this role require of me?
3. How do I act with friends outside the classroom? Do I act

the same way with all of my friends? If not, why do I act differently? How does the age of the people I am with affect my actions?

4. If I am a boy, how do I act differently with other boys than I do with girls? How do I act with a special girl? If I am a girl, do I act differently with other girls than I do with boys? How do I act with a special boy? (It will be useful to remember the discussion and writing you did on this topic for Chapter 6.) How much of the role is imposed by society? How much is determined by the individual?

5. What roles that I have to play do I find difficult or unpleasant? Why? Do they become less difficult the more often I play them? If so, how? If not, why not?

Discovering as much about yourself and your roles as you possibly can is very helpful in learning to project yourself through your writing and to assume various roles as a writer.

Writing Assignment 1

In groups of from three to five students, prepare a one-act play on a controversial subject or a point of conflict in which each character has a distinct point of view and is in direct conflict with at least one of the other characters. As a group, decide upon the situation and the characters; then decide which writer will be responsible for which character. It will be necessary to work together throughout this assignment as the lines for each character will have to mesh with the others to create the dramatic incident. After the play is written, present it to the class with each writer portraying the role he has created.

Decide on an incident in which some sort of conflict is present. Some of the following situations may give you some ideas, but you need not use any of them.

1. A conflict between a teen-age boy or girl and his or her mother and father over dating, drinking, the use of the car, a major purchase, going or not going to college, and so forth.

2. A conflict over some issue involving people of different races and/or social positions.

3. A conflict over some ecological issue among people of various interest groups, such as a politician, a manufacturer, a leader of a conservation group, a scientist, and a concerned citizen.
4. A conflict among a group of teen-agers over some issue or problem involving a school-related activity, church-related activity, or social activity.
5. A heated discussion among several people involving politics, religion, marriage, or war.

After your group has decided upon the subject of the play and who the characters (and the creator of each) will be, investigate the range of points of view that might be represented by the different characters. Then isolate the significant characteristics of each character and the attitudes that would most probably stem from his point of view.

1. Is the character male or female? Will this play a significant part in determining the person's point of view on this subject?
2. How old is the character? What effect will this have on his point of view and his interaction with the other people?
3. How will the race, religion, and cultural background of the character affect his point of view? How will it affect the way he responds to the other characters and the way they respond to him?
4. Does the character have a vested interest in the problem causing the conflict? If so, what is it and how does it affect his point of view?
5. What other experiences or lack of experiences affect the character's point of view and the judgment expressed by the other characters of his opinions?
6. What emotional and intellectual attributes will be assigned to each character? Is he emotional, calm, involved, or detached? Highly intelligent? Of average intelligence? How much formal education does the character have? How does this affect his point of view?
7. How will I convey all of these things through dialogue alone?

After your group has discussed these questions and come up with some answers, you might want to assume your assigned roles and act out the situation without a script, letting your responses come spontaneously as the situation develops. It would be most beneficial to have a tape recording of this original performance to listen to and to transcribe if necessary. The enactment and a discussion of it can serve as a basis for the actual preparation of the script.

As you and the rest of the group write your script, keep in mind the problem you are dramatizing and the personalities of the characters involved in the conflict. Remember that in a drama almost everything has to be conveyed through dialogue and action; what the character says and does must reveal to the audience what he is thinking and feeling as well as show them the significant influences that are operating to shape his point of view.

Pay particular attention to the ideas that you have each character express and also to the language he uses to express those ideas, since, as we have said, language must carry so much of the total burden of conveying the conflict. After you have written an initial draft of the play, look carefully at the dialogue of each character and as a group ask such questions as the following:

1. Does the dialogue sound like real people talking? Does the language of each character fit him? Is his language consistent throughout? Is his point of view realistic? Is it consistent throughout? If his language or point of view shifts, does it do so for a good reason, or is this a weakness in the script?
2. Have I created a realistic, believable character? Are the reasons for who and what he is evident to the audience? Is he doing and saying things in the situation that an actual person with his point of view might do or say?
3. Are the distinct points of view and the reasons for each obvious to the audience? Will the audience believe in the possibility of such a conflict, and will they understand from the dialogue and action why the characters are in conflict?

In addition to the problems posed by such questions, it will be necessary for your group to think about the effectiveness of your play as drama. Will it catch and hold the interest of an audience? Do the dialogue and action move smoothly and swiftly?

Your original performance without a script should have helped to create accurate and realistic dialogue. As you write and rewrite, you should act out the play among yourselves, listening closely to the lines and making changes, additions, and deletions where necessary.

When the script is completed, it should be presented as a play, with the actors playing the roles without a script and, perhaps, with some elementary props. If that is not possible, then a dramatic reading using scripts and only suggesting actions and props will suffice.

After each presentation the class should discuss the effectiveness of the play, considering especially the various points of view expressed and the ways in which the language and actions of each character expressed his point of view. Consider such questions as: How does the drama convey the influences that have helped to shape the ideas and attitudes of each character? How does each character's response in this situation indicate his point of view?

DRAMA AND FICTION

Dramatization is a most effective way to portray human thoughts and deeds. Of all forms of literature, perhaps it comes closest to real life. Yet the ability of drama to approximate real life also imposes upon it one particular limitation—a limitation also present in our own lives. That is, how do we know what people are actually thinking? In real life it is impossible to know; we can only guess what people are thinking and feeling through observing their actions and listening to their words. The dramatist is faced with the same problem. He must convey everything through word and deed.

The writer of fiction, however, can take us into the minds of his characters if he chooses. He can describe not only what his characters are saying and doing, but also what they are thinking and feeling—but not necessarily expressing. The writer of fiction can choose a narrator who can see into the minds of the characters and report what is going on in there. This kind of all-knowing narrator is referred to as an omniscient narrator.

While writing your play, you may have found it difficult to convey everything about each character through his speech and actions. Unless you had the character say some things aloud to the other people that he would be unlikely to say in real life, you had to be content to imply and suggest what the character was thinking.

Writing Assignment 2

After you have had the opportunity to present your play to the class, discuss it with them and think about it in terms of the preceding discussion of the strengths and weaknesses of drama as a device for conveying point of view. Then rework your play into a short story in which you act as an omniscient narrator—a narrator who can and does look into the minds of all the characters.

This writing assignment should not be done in a group. Each member of each group should write the story entirely on his own, without consulting the members of his original group.

Your task is to translate the action and dialogue of the play into a short story. You will now be able to give the reader additional insights into the characters by conveying not only what they are saying and doing, but also what they are thinking. In addition, you may want to tell the reader something about each character's past that is significant to the incident covered in the story. Determining how much of this kind of information is necessary and desirable without interfering with the movement of the story will be one of the decisions you will have to make as a writer.

As you prepare to write, and while you are writing and revising, you should probably consider questions such as the following:

1. What do I have to tell the reader of a short story that would be obvious to him when the story is presented in the form of a play? (Consider the sets, props, and costumes in a play, for instance. How are these things handled in a short story?)
2. If I tell about the character's background and previous experiences, do I have to tell something about every character? How do I decide?
3. What will each character be thinking and feeling? How much of this will be conveyed through dialogue and how

much through description of the action? How will I convey these thoughts to the reader? Will I tell the reader all the thoughts going through the mind of each character or will I hold some back? How will I decide?

4. Do I want to make one character more admirable than the others? If so, why? How can I do this? If I want to present all the characters as objectively as possible and let the reader make up his mind about them, how can I best do that?

5. What kind of voice will I use as the narrator? Will I be as unobtrusive as possible, or will I assume a definite personality and character? Will I deliberately attempt to sway the reader's opinions and reactions, or will I try to interfere as little as possible with his opinions and reactions? What words will I use when I am speaking as the narrator? Will they be different from the language of the characters? Will each character speak differently than the others? Will the thoughts of each character be expressed in essentially the same language as his speech? If there are differences, what should they be and why?

Such questions should help you to see the advantages and the difficulties of omniscience. Even when you have an opportunity to know everything, you still must decide what you know and why. Then you must decide what you are going to tell and how and why you are going to tell it.

After you have completed your story, exchange it with the other members of your original playwriting group. If possible, have all the papers duplicated so that each of you will have a copy of each story to read, compare, and comment upon. *Do not identify the writer of each story.* Do not identify yourself as the writer during the discussion.

After you have had an opportunity to read and think about each of the stories, discuss them with the other people in your group. Compare the various treatments of the story and characters. Consider especially the thoughts each writer has placed in the mind of each character and the kind of person that each writer has made of each character.

1. Has each writer handled each character in essentially the same way? Or have some characters been portrayed very differently by different writers? If so, how and why do

characters differ? Which story is most effective? Why?

2. Which character is most effectively portrayed in all the stories? Which character is least effectively portrayed in the stories? Why? Was one character especially troublesome for all the writers? What seem to be the reasons?

Your analysis, discussion, and comparison of the various stories can tell you many things about your effectiveness as a writer in capturing and conveying different points of view. A German writer, Jean Paul Richter, once wrote: "A man never reveals his character more vividly than when portraying the character of another." In this sequence of assignments, you have had the opportunity to portray and speak through other characters. And the differences in the way the characters were portrayed by the various writers in your group may have revealed something about each of you—something you may not have been aware of yourself.

Look carefully at each of the stories and attempt to determine who wrote each one. Is there something in the characterization, the language, the treatment of the story that offers clues (mostly unintentional) to the identity of the writer? Support your conclusion by citing evidence from the story and relating it to what you think you know and actually do know about the supposed writer. Then return to your groups to compare your conclusions. Your analysis, whether correct or incorrect, can reveal something not only about the others, but also about yourself. After every person in the group has presented his analysis and conclusion, each writer should identify himself. Discuss the reasons for the success or failure of your conclusions.

Writing Assignment 3

Oscar Wilde, the British writer of fiction, poetry, and drama, wrote: "Man is least himself when he talks in his own person. Give him a *mask* and he will tell the truth."

You are hereby given a mask to conceal your identity. "Tell the truth."

Write a paper in which you will be entirely anonymous as a writer and in which you will tell the truth about something you ordinarily would not talk about or would be hesitant to talk about in your own voice. Identify your paper by some code so that you will know that it is yours; you will not have to reveal yourself even to the teacher. Tell the truth as you see it as honestly, as forcefully, and as clearly as you can. Your classmates will be your audience unless you indicate otherwise.

After the papers have been written, they should be collected in such a way as to protect the identity of the writer. Then you should select a paper at random from the pile. If you should happen to get your own, return it and select another.

Write, again anonymously, your honest response to the paper you have drawn. Is it truthful? Is it effectively written? Do you agree or disagree? Why or why not? Attach your paper to the one you have responded to and return both to the teacher. After the teacher has read them, he or she can choose a few for duplication and distribution to the class. After everyone has had a chance to read these papers, they should be discussed by the class.

Consider such questions as the following:

1. Does each paper tell the "truth"? If so, why do I think so? If not, why not?
2. Does each paper tell the "truth" effectively? Why or why not?
3. Which is the more truthful of each set, the original or the response? Why? Which of the two is most effective in telling the truth? Why and how?
4. What is the point of view of each writer? How does that point of view influence his conception of what is true? How do the influences upon my point of view affect the way I respond to his "truth?"
5. Do I think the writer would have seen and/or told the same "truth" without his mask? Why or why not? Is having a mask actually having another point of view? Explain.
6. Based on the discussion and the evidence of the papers themselves, is the Oscar Wilde quotation true? Why or why not?

Chapter 11

A Funny Thing Happened to My Point of View

Comedians, humorists, and satirists frequently view the world from unexpected points of view—their humor depends upon their audience's realization that they are looking at the world through another's eyes or commenting on people from a different point of view. For example, Flip Wilson, arrayed in dress and wig, amuses audiences with the antics of "Geraldine," his scatterbrained creation. Dressed like a hobo and mimicking what he considers to be a hobo's mannerisms and speech, Red Skelton has entertained audiences for years as "Freddie the Freeloader."

Television comics frequently impersonate the mannerisms of celebrities while commenting on something that the audience would normally not expect from the celebrity. For example, a comic might imitate the language and actions of the President of the United States while talking about a football game, or women's fashions, or a traffic ticket.

In the following article from a daily newspaper, Russell Baker looks at Little Miss Muffet from eight different points of view.

Curds of Opinion, Miss Muffet, a Tuffet, and Scientific Whey

by Russell Baker

WASHINGTON—Little Miss Muffet, as everyone knows, sat on a tuffet eating her curds and whey when along came a spider who sat down beside her and frightened Miss Muffet away. While everyone knows it, the significance of the event had never been analyzed until a conference of thinkers recently brought their special insights to bear upon it. Following are excerpts from the transcript of their discussion:

Sociologist: We are clearly dealing with a prototypical illustration of a highly tensile social structure's tendency to dis- or perhaps even de-structure itself under the pressures created when optimum minimums do not obtain among the disadvantaged. Miss Muffet is nutritionally underprivileged, as evidenced by the subminimal diet of curds and whey upon which she is forced to subsist, while the spider's cultural disadvantage is evidenced by such phenomena as legs exceeding standard norms, odd mating habits and so forth.

In this instance, spider expectations lead the culturally disadvantaged to assert demands to share the tuffet with the nutritionally underprivileged. Due to a communications failure, Miss Muffet assumes without evidence that the spider will not be satisfied to share her tuffet, but will also insist on eating her curds and whey. Thus, the failure to pre-establish selectively optimum norm structures leads to. . . .

Militarist: Second-strike capability, sir; that's what was lacking. If Miss Muffet had developed a second-strike capability instead of squandering her resources on curds and whey, no spider on earth would have dared launch a first strike capable of carrying him right to the heart of her tuffet. I am confident that Miss Muffet had adequate notice from experts that she could not afford both curds and whey and at the same time support an Early Spider Warning system. Yet curds alone were not good enough for Miss Muffet, she had to have whey, too. Tuffet security must be the first responsibility of every diner. . . .

Book Reviewer: Written on several levels, this searing, sensitive exploration of the arachnid heart illuminates the agony and splendor of Jewish family life with a candor that is at once breathtaking in its simplicity and soul-shattering in its implied ambiguity. Some will doubtless be shocked to see such subjects as tuffets and whey discussed without flinching, but hereafter writers too timid to call a tuffet will no longer. . . .

Editorial Writer: Why has the government not seen fit to tell the public all it knows about the so-called curds-and-whey affair? It is not enough to suggest that this was merely a random incident involving a lonely spider and a young diner. In today's world, poised as it is on the knife edge of. . . .

Psychiatrist: Little Miss Muffet is, of course, neither little nor a miss. These are obviously the self she has created in her own fantasies to escape the reality that she is a gross divorcee whose superego makes it impossible for her to sustain a normal relationship with any man, symbolized by the spider, who, of course, has no existence outside her fantasies. She may, in fact, be a man with deeply repressed oedipal impulses who sees in the spider the father he would like to kill, and very well may some day unless he admits that what he believes to be a tuffet is, in fact, probably the dining room chandelier and that the whey he thinks he is eating is, in fact probably. . . .

Flower Child: This beautiful kid is on a bad trip. Like. . . .

Student Demonstrator: Little Miss Muffet, tuffets, curds, whey and spiders are what's wrong with education today. They're all irrelevant. Tuffets are irrelevant. Curds are irrelevant. Whey is irrelevant, without meaningful experience! How can you have relevance without meaningful experience? And how can there ever be meaningful experience without understanding? With understanding and meaningfulness and relevance, there can be love and good and deep seriousness, and education today will be freed of slavery and Little Miss Muffet, and life will become meaningful. . . .

Child: But this is about a little girl who gets scared by a spider.

Discussion

1. Did you find Mr. Baker's article amusing? Why or why not?
2. How did he create the eight points of view? Was his language for each realistic? Why or why not?

Writing Assignment 1

Examine something with which you are familiar, such as a game, a toy, a book, a children's story, a recent event that made the news, or an announcement from a school official or a city official. Then react to that object or event as you think five or six different people would. For example, how do you think the following might view a high school football game?

a Russian diplomat
a member of the local Humane Society
a mother of one of the players
a psychiatrist
a hippie
a retired pro-football quarterback
a student sportscaster
a foreigner who has never seen a football game
an expert chess player
an Army officer
a poet
a doctor

If you attempted to view the game of football humorously from five or six of these points of view, what would you have to know about each of the people you selected to make your account funny?

Your task here is to write about anything from five or six distinct points of view. Your purpose is to make your audience —your classmates—laugh.

There's Only One Catch

In the following excerpt from his best-selling novel *Catch-22*, Joseph Heller examines military life from a fresh point of view.

It was a horrible joke, but Doc Daneeka didn't laugh until Yossarian came to him one mission later and pleaded again, without any real expectation of success, to be grounded. Doc Daneeka snickered once and was soon immersed in problems of his own, which included Chief White Halfoat, who had been challenging him all that morning to Indian wrestle, and Yossarian, who decided right then and there to go crazy.

"You're wasting your time," Doc Daneeka was forced to tell him.

"Can't you ground someone's who's crazy?"

"Oh, sure. I have to. There's a rule saying I have to ground anyone who's crazy."

"Then why don't you ground me? I'm crazy. Ask Clevinger."

"Clevinger? Where *is* Clevinger? You find Clevinger and I'll ask him."

"Then ask any of the others. They'll tell you how crazy I am."

"They're crazy."

"Then why don't you ground them?"

"Why don't they ask me to ground them?"

"Because they're crazy, that's why."

"Of course, they're crazy," Doc Daneeka replied. "I just told you they're crazy, didn't I? And you can't let crazy people decide whether you're crazy or not, can you?"

Yossarian looked at him soberly and tried another approach. "Is Orr crazy?"

"He sure is," Doc Daneeka said.

"Can you ground him?"

"I sure can. But first he has to ask me to. That's part of the rule."

"Then why doesn't he ask you to?"

"Because he's crazy," Doc Daneeka said. "He has to be crazy to keep flying combat missions after all the close calls he's had. Sure, I can ground Orr. But first he has to ask me to."

"That's all he has to do to be grounded?"

"That's all. Let him ask me."

"And then you can ground him?" Yossarian asked.

"No. Then I can't ground him."

"You mean there's a catch?"

"Sure there's a catch," Doc Daneeka replied. "Catch-

22. Anyone who wants to get out of combat duty isn't really crazy."

There was only one catch and that was Catch-22, which specified that a concern for one's own safety in the face of dangers that were real and immediate was the process of a rational mind. Orr was crazy and could be grounded. All he had to do was ask and as soon as he did, he would no longer be crazy and would have to fly more missions. Orr would be crazy to fly more missions and sane if he didn't, but if he was sane he had to fly them. If he flew them he was crazy and didn't have to; but if he didn't want to he was sane and had to. Yossarian was moved very deeply by the absolute simplicity of this clause of Catch-22 and let out a respectful whistle.

"That's some catch, that Catch-22," he observed.

"It's the best there is," Doc Daneeka agreed.

Discussion

1. Why is Catch-22 "the best there is," according to Doc Daneeka?
2. Why do you think this passage from *Catch-22* is, or is not, humorous? If you think it is, what devices does Mr. Heller use to make it humorous?
3. Is this passage believable? Explain your answer. What rules and regulations in your life could be treated in somewhat the same manner as Mr. Heller treats Catch-22?

Writing Assignment 2

Examine some of the rules and regulations that you have to live with daily. Can any of them be treated humorously? Why or why not?

If you decide that you know of no rule or regulation that can be treated humorously, consider the following:

"Where are you going?" the hall monitor barked.
"To the principal's office," I replied.
"What for?"
"To get a hall pass."
"Where's your hall pass?"
"I'm going to get one."

"Are you out in the hall without a pass?"

"I'm going to get one."

"Go back to your classroom. You can't be out in the hall without a pass."

"I know; that's why I'm going to the principal's office to get a pass."

"But you can't be out in the hall without a pass."

"But I'm going . . ."

"Back to the classroom!"

Has something like that ever happened to you? What did you do? What did the other person do? How did he defend the rule? Who won? Why?

Or perhaps you applied for a job and were turned down because you lacked experience.

"How do I get experience," you asked, "if no one will hire me so that I can get some experience?"

"I don't know," the man said. "That's a real problem"

The professional humorist pokes fun at nearly everything. He looks at the world and the people in it with a twinkle in his eye, waiting to find something that will amuse him. Art Buchwald, the syndicated newspaper columnist, is one of the most popular of the present-day humorists. His humor is satirical, his targets are everyone and everything. He unleashes his devastating wit on presidents and premiers, customs and fashions, world crises and worldwide idiocies. The following column reveals the typical Buchwald wit.

"Hey Tovarich, Honey: The Fashion Gap is Showing"

by Art Buchwald

"Comrade buyers, fashion designers and state managers of state department stores. Is honor to introduce Comrade Torkel, who has just completed visit to America where he has observed new fashions now being worn on American women. Comrade Torkel."

"Is pleasure to be back in Moscow, comrades, and give report on American fashions with illustrations from magazines.

"Here, comrades, is first dress. Skirt is coming to below knees."

"But, Comrade Torkel, we've been making this dress in Leningrad dress factory for 20 years. What is new about this?"

"Am only reporting what have seen. Here second illustration. Evening pajamas to go to party in."

"You are mad, Comrade Torkel. Why would American women go to parties in their pajamas when they are richest women in world?"

"Is impossible to explain, but every reception I went to, I saw women wearing pajamas."

"But Comrade Torkel, if American women wear pajamas to party, what do they wear to bed?"

"Is nothing."

"Nothing?"

"Is called 'new permissiveness.' Now, comrades, here is woman in pants suit."

"Are those for women railroad workers?"

"No, comrades, those are for women to go to restaurants, cocktails and dinner."

"COMRADE TORKEL, you are making fun of us. How can women wear pants in America when not working in factory?"

"Is being done all over."

"The Kiev Pants Cooperative has been making pants like that since the revolution."

"Is true. Now here is outfit women wear to go out shopping in. Is leather coat with leather boots and fur on collar."

"But, Comrade Torkel, this woman looks like a member of the Communist Party."

"She could be working for KGB."

"Is true. Leather coats and boots are now the fashion."

"The GUM Department Store in Moscow had this outfit 10 years ago. We were stuck with hundreds of them."

"Next illustration. Here is peasant blouse and peasant skirt and no shoes for afternoon wear."

"But that is what they have been wearing in Smolensk since Stalin died."

"My sister, Katrina, wore an outfit like that until she got a job."

"And here, comrades, is the *pièce de résistance*. Is

knickers with boots and woolen sweater and woolen hat."

"Comrade Torkel, do they have women Cossacks in America?"

"No Cossacks. Is for going to beauty parlor and night clubs."

"To think Malinkock was sent to Siberia when his factory once tried to make knickers and they wouldn't sell."

"What are your conclusions, Comrade Torkel?"

"Is obvious, comrades, that American women want to look like Russian women. We also know Russian women all want to look the way American women *used* to look. Is possible we make barter deal. We give them all the clothes our women won't wear that we make; they give us all the clothes their women refuse to wear now."

"Comrade Torkel, is fantastic solution to our rotten clothes problem. I am putting you in for the Lenin Medal today."

Instead of our preparing a set of questions on Buchwald's column, we ask you to do so. What questions would you ask your classmates that would call their attention to Buchwald's humor without spoiling it for them? Prepare a set of questions that will help a student better understand how and why Buchwald's humor works.

Writing Assignment 3

The authors hope you have enjoyed some of the writing assignments in this book. We have prepared a number for you; now it is your turn. What assignment would you give us? What instructions would you give? How would you satirize our assignments?

Your final task is to prepare a writing assignment for the authors of this book that deals with some aspect of point of view. Be imaginative. Be inventive. Be realistic. But before you go all out, reread some of the assignments carefully so that you can treat yours humorously.

A 1
B 2
C 3
D 4
E 5
F 6
G 7
H 8
I 9
J 0